Soaring Solo

*On the Joys (yes, joys!)
of Being a Single Mother*

Wendy Keller

T0164246

Wildcat Canyon Press
A Division of Circulus Publishing Group, Inc.
Berkeley, California

Soaring Solo: On the Joys (yes, joys!) of Being a Single Mother

Publisher: Tamara Traeder
Editorial Director: Roy M. Carlisle
Marketing Director: Carol Brown
Managing Editor: Leyza Yardley
Production Coordinator: Larissa Berry
Copyeditor: Megan Hiller
Proofreader: Shirley Coe
Cover Design: Mary Beth Salmon
Interior Design and Typesetting: A Page Turner

Typographic Specifications: Text in Goudy 11/14, headings in Balzano.

Printed in the United States of America

Library of Congress Cataloguing-in-Publication Data
Keller, Wendy, 1964-
    Soaring solo: on the Joys (yes, joys!) of being a single mother/Wendy Keller.
        p. cm.
    Includes bibliographical references.
    ISBN 1-885171-60-9 (alk. paper)
    1. Single mothers—United States. 2. Single-parent families. I. Title.
HQ759.915 K455 2001
306.874'3—dc21

                                                        00-068594

Distributed to the trade by Publishers Group West

10 9 8 7 6 5 4 3 2 1

Soaring Solo

*For my precious daughter, Sophia Rose,
Who taught me everything I know
about single motherhood*

Acknowledgments

No book is ever completed without a vast team of people behind the scenes. Like every author, I owe gratitude to everyone from the secretary at my publisher's office to the bookstore person who tells a customer how great this book is. I am thankful to everyone who is part of this process, but I especially wish to thank:

Roy M. Carlisle, who is so much more than a wonderful editor to me,

My mother, Carol Keller, for teaching me so much about parenting,

And you, my reader. I hope these words will comfort you, inspire you, support you, make you laugh and cry, and most of all, remind you to savor each moment of your life as it is now, where you are now, as your child grows.

Editorial Note

There are some very personal stories in this book, shared by brave and open women who wanted to tell the truth about their struggles and triumphs as single moms. In the name of their privacy, I have changed the names of everyone in this book, except my own and my child's. I suspect that in many cases, you could replace the name I made up with your own, and the story could be yours. Our journey is similar—proof we really are all in this together. Our love and support of other women is the bond that holds the world gently together.

Contents

A Word about Motherhood 10

It's a Dog's Life 14

Tiffany's Mother's Box of Love 18

Lizzy's Hair 21

The Amazing Mrs. Kenna 24

Motivating the Troops 27

Balancing Act 31

Givers Gain 35

Teetering on the Totter 37

Starry Eyes 40

Penelope and the Guilt-O-Meter 44

Am I Doing This Right? 47

Green Rivers of Cash 51

Mrs. Potash, The Martyr of Maryland 56

The Power of One 59

Single Dads 63

For the Love of Money 66

Rocks for Sale 69

The Surprising Return 72

Graduation Day 75

Knocking Up Opportunity 79

Dark Night of the Soul 82

Cash on the Barrel Head 86

The Road to Truth 89

A Blizzard of Bliss 92

Instant Parenting: Just Add Water 94

Squid Factor 99
One Who Kisses 103
Parallel Lives 107
I'll Leave the Light On for Ya 112
Time to Fly 115
The Wedding Dress 118
Crying in the Dark 121
The Hamster of Happiness 126
The Collection 129
Finding Your Creative Spirit 132
Loving Your Body 135
Just Say No in Minneapolis 138
Less Is More Toast 141
Homework Wars 145
Small Moments 148
Flow, Names that Cannot Be Pronounced Easily,
    and Doing Things You Hate To Do 151
Christmas Cookies 154
Good-Bye, Happily Ever After 158
One More Push 161
Secret Wishes 164
Starting Over, Again 167
Finding Joy 169
Brave Heart 172
Sleeping Beauty 174
Sleep Softly and Carry a Big Stick 176
Boarding School Blues 180
Tick, Tock, Biological Clock 183
I Like Myself! I Like Myself! 185

Yellow Cab 188
Dealing with Dear Old Dad 191
If It Ain't Dirty, Don't Wash It 194
Girls Just Wanna Have Fun 197
Me and the Boyz 199
A Little Bit of Sunshine 202
Daddy's Gone 204
Dating Again 207
On Living Single 210
Flab, Stretch Marks, and Me 214
The Sky's The Limit! 218

Bibliography 222
A Note from the Author 223
About the Author 223
About the Press 224

A Word about Motherhood

The greatest love is a mother's, then a dog's, then a sweetheart's. —Polish proverb

The hand that rocks the cradle rules the world.
—German proverb

The foundations of eternity are laid in the nursery. —WK

Before I had children, I had six theories on how they should be raised. Now I have five children and no theories.
—Ronald Kelly, minister, father

The very word "motherhood" conjures up a thousand pictures in our heads. The famous portraits of Mother and Child, the ideals we had for our children when they were small, the plans we made for our beloved child when we were pregnant, even sometimes ideas we had about what motherhood would be like from the vantage point of our teenage years.

Some of us swore we'd do it differently than our mothers had, and others wanted to be similar in our style. Some of us wished to marry and have babies when we were grown ups, and others wanted to postpone babies, maybe indefinitely, while we cured cancer or made millions or showed men how powerful we really are.

Our attitudes about motherhood change as we have children and with the circumstances of their births and lives. You may be finding that the ideal life you'd planned to provide your child is a little harder to provide than you'd hoped, or even that the child you got isn't quite the child you expected. You may find, like most of us do, that motherhood and parenthood in general are experiences beyond description, so much better and so very different than anything you'd planned on.

Motherhood is mysterious, magical, a whirl of drudgery and joy, carpools and kid caresses, sleepless nights and peak moments, the greatest joys, and the deepest sorrows. It is every emotion in the spectrum and every thought of selfless love that ever existed in the universe. Some say it is the closest thing to pure love that exists on Earth.

But isn't it funny how life turns out? I wanted a ballerina and I got a tomboy. Megan up the block was sure she'd get a singer, and instead she got a budding actor with almost no musical skills. Barry's son was supposed to follow Dad into the law. At twenty-seven, he shows no signs of following. They're their own little people, aren't they? So what does that make our job?

Remember when your mother wished on you a child just like yourself? Maybe you got that kid, and maybe not, and maybe that was a blessing from your mom, but maybe it was a curse. Either way, here you are, in the circumstances of your life as it is today. Here you are with your kid(s) in your house with your job and your life, and if you are doing this all alone, then it is all up to you.

Like everything else, that's a blessing and a curse. You have the liberty to craft the mind, heart, self-esteem, and virtues of the child entrusted to your care. You also have all the responsibility to provide structure, discipline, meals, clothes, a roof, and a warm bed for this little person.

When life doesn't match your expectations, when the "Happily Ever After" ends and the next chapter of your life begins, it's easy to forget the most important things. It's easy to forget there is joy in the simple fact that you are alive and you have a good mind. It's possible to forget for a moment that you are in control of your circumstances and that at any point you can create a whole new kind of tomorrow for your family. In any moment, there are things to be sad about and things to rejoice about. Your quality of life will be enhanced by remembering to celebrate the joys of single motherhood and soaring above it on the wings of your sometimes-angelic children.

Motherhood is a brief and precious time in our lives. Ask any woman, married or single, who has raised a family and watched each child fly the nest. She'll tell you it doesn't really last long, it just seems like it when you can't sleep through the night that first year, or when you and your child wage daily skirmishes. The period from birth to college or their first apartment seems like a long time, but in retrospect went like a flash. This little human being we've been given, with all her or his uniqueness, perfections, and imperfections, is ours to hold, ours to mold, for such a little while. Cherish that time!

You've heard "The hand that rocks the cradle rules the world." Your child's destiny is in your power. Will you craft a neurotic little being who is a tyrant over the other people in his life? Will you indulge a spoiled child who grows up to embarrass you? Or will you set the plan, stay the course, be there with an open heart and open arms, nurturing, supporting, and loving this person who has been given into your care?

The time when we have influence over our children is terribly short. It's a solar flare on the timescape of our existence. The foundations of eternity are laid in the nursery. The kind of mother you are capable of being at your best is precisely the kind of mother your child needs. Here's to you, for caring enough to be the very best.

It's a Dog's Life

It's a dog-eat-dog world, and I'm wearing milk bone shorts.
—Kelly Allen

*Cats are smarter than dogs. You can't get eight cats to pull a
sled through the snow.*
—Jeff Valdez

One hot, sticky, gritty summer night in Los Angeles, under
the grapevine in the backyard, our four-year-old cocker
spaniel, Sabatchka ("Little Dog" in Russian), gave birth to
puppies. I didn't know then that she would teach me, the
mother of two, how to take care of children. But she did.

Since it was hot, I decided to bring her into the nice,
cool, air-conditioned house while she labored. I made a
special nest out of an old cardboard box and some clean
rags. Then I went out and very gently carried in my labor-
ing dog and her first two puppies. I set the little family in
the box and soon was rewarded with a third puppy. I left
Sabatchka in peace for about half an hour. When I returned
to the laundry room, the nest was empty!

Back under the grapevine, I found my dog with four
puppies rooting around for their first meal in the nest she'd
chosen, the one she'd made for herself. I determined to
leave her there and go to bed. Mother knows best, even if
mother is an eleven-pound mutt.

The next morning, I found six puppies and their mother
sleeping in the nest under the bright, soft leaves.

Puppies grow fast, and they eat about two hundred times a day, or so it must have seemed to my dog. She ate voraciously to supply the brood with the milk they needed. As I nursed my infant daughter, I watched Sabatchka's puppies crawling all over their mother, clambering for milk.

I'd been told having two children is much more than twice the work of having just one, but I doubted this could be true. Now in the thick of raising a three-year-old and a new baby, I was exhausted. I knew that it was important to be a Good Mother. I knew that women on TV managed to have the house clean, the kids fed and ready for bed, a baby sleeping through the night from birth, and themselves in a negligee when the husband comes in the door in the evening. I did my best to try to create this image in my home.

Somehow, my best intentions were foiled by two car seats and screaming tantrums at the grocery store and sleepless nights and ear infections and playing trucks with a baby in my other arm and walks to push a swing at the park while the baby snoozed in a backpack and dishes, always dirty.

Postpartum depression swamped me a few months later. I was sitting in what had been my office, what would be my office again when I was past "the rough part." I was feeling sorry for myself—this was so much work! I was feeling inadequate and tired and fat and ugly and like I was losing my mind. I plopped down in the desk chair and tossed my house-slippered feet up on the desk in defeat. I was feeling guilty for not keeping up, overwhelmed by all the things on my To Do list, and simply exhausted. I just needed two minutes, and then I'd start cleaning up the morning's tornado of toys.

And then it happened.

I looked out on the patio, where poor Sabatchka was raising her six puppies. The puppies were standing in a whining, yelping, whimpering circle, desperately clawing at the brick barbecue. They were scratching at the bricks, with all their effort trying to find a way to climb to the first ledge. All of them were begging in dog language for help getting up to the ledge.

Because there, in the center of the ledge, napping in the sun, was their exhausted mother. This little eleven-pound dog was rejuvenating herself, and the kids, well, they'd just have to wait. I'm sure she could hear them whining. I'm sure she knew that she'd eventually have to come down and feed them all for the fifteenth time that hour. But her instincts told her to take a break, that it was okay, that she deserved and needed a rest.

I decided to start trusting my own instincts that very day.

Now when I'm worn out with mothering, or tuckered out from sitting at that desk talking to clients on the phone all day, I let myself take a break. This has become more important than ever in the half dozen years I've been a single mom. In this time, I've learned that if I don't take care of me, then just like poor Sabatchka, nobody else will either.

The irony of taking time for myself is this: When I do come back to motherhood or work after a short break, I feel rested, more peaceful, and calmer. I'm able to cope with things that just twenty minutes ago were bending me to the breaking point. A friend recently told me he's learned that true peace and calm is being able to accept winning or losing $50,000 with perfect equanimity. I'm not there yet.

The Myth of the Perfect Mother permeates our culture. Single Moms can be the worst victims of this myth, especially if they are already feeling guilty over how much they work or that their children don't have a "real" father—whatever that means.

We assume that using up all our personal resources means we are helping our children. What we are doing is setting an example of a woman who doesn't know her own boundaries and limitations. Take it easy on yourself this week—you won't shirk your responsibilities—and watch and see whether you don't return to your duties rejuvenated, refreshed, and better able to cope more calmly than when you were burning yourself out trying to be Super Mom.

Tiffany's Mother's Box of Love

In this life, we cannot do great things. We can only do small things with great love. —Mother Teresa, *as quoted in* Lighting a Candle

No one has ever loved anyone the way everyone wants to be loved. —Mignon McLaughlin, *author*

If you asked me I would have said when she and I were college sophomores, Tiffany was a dingbat. She wore polka-dot dresses and ridiculous bows in her long California-blond hair. Her daddy was a hot shot realtor, her mom the hothouse variety of housewife. Their cosseted daughter belonged to a sorority, got her nails done in a salon, and went to exotic places on summer break. I was so jealous I could have spit. But not really about all that.

We struck up a sort of friendship in Advanced French class. She was better than me at French, which I admired. She befriended me, I think, because she perceived herself as helping the lower classes in the traditional Grand dame style. That didn't endear her to me, but what *did* impress me about this young woman, and what did intrigue me enough to make me want to hang around her, was her mother.

Yep, her mother. A woman I never met and surely wouldn't have liked if I had.

Her mother thought that they were starving her little darling in that over-furnished sorority house. So she'd send Tiffany care packages every single week. Every week. Without fail. And bigger ones on critical holidays like St. Patrick's Day and Groundhog's Day. Once she had a whole bunch of plants delivered to the dorm room, just to brighten the place up for her precious child. Tiffany didn't water them, and they all died.

Her mom would stuff in love letters and boxes of candy or crackers and cheese and school supplies and new clothes, and if she thought it needed packing peanuts, she'd fill the rest of the box with popcorn she popped herself. Or more likely, had the maid pop for her.

Tiffany always had an enormous supply of stale popcorn in her room, because by the time it got to our college it was always stale. We didn't care. I'd come over and she'd share the contents of her care packages. Sometimes she'd read the letters aloud. I always made fun of them and her, to her face and behind her back. (Twenty years ago, I had a long way to go to learn to be nice.) Sometimes we'd even eat the popcorn, but mostly we just talked.

At dinner hour, I'd walk home to my general purpose cheapest-housing-on-campus girls' dorm with the regulation greenish-yellow walls and detached noises, and I'd feel so jealous and forlorn I'd want to cry. I couldn't quite explain it back then, but now I can.

I was jealous that her mother took the time every single week to show her youngest daughter how much she loved her. Here I was, a "young adult," and I was jealous of stale popcorn and the love that filled the air gaps around each kernel.

As our children grow, I've observed that we often think they are "too old" for silly stuff like kisses or little notes or gifts. They balk and make fun of us for trying to be loving. Our attempts to cuddle a thirteen-year-old boy or have a nice day with an adolescent girl are sometimes thwarted by our child, so we give up in despair and stop trying.

Tiffany appreciated her mother's attentions. Through the window of time passed, I see that some would accuse them of being obsessive about each other. But in the lives of two lonely girls away from home, it meant a lot to both of us that her mother cared that much about her.

When my eight-year-old becomes old enough to leave me for summer camp or college or the peace corps or wherever she chooses to go, I'm going to continue loving her and doing nice things that no one else would even attempt—whether she thinks it is annoying or not.

Giving love is the responsibility of the giver. How it is received or later perceived is not the giver's responsibility. To be consistently loving to a child, with a strong enough sense of one's own self to not use it in a vain attempt to manipulate a child and wrest love for ourselves, is the greatest gift of all.

Lizzy's Hair

*Sacred refers to that which helps take us out of our little selves
and into the whole mountains-and-rivers mandala universe.*
—Gary Snyder, author

*You can't depend on your eyes when your imagination is out of
focus.* —Mark Twain, author

A woman named Lizzy lives in my little town. Lizzy is also
a single mother, as we found out once when our girls were
swinging side by side in the local park. The girls became
friends and so did we. We share the ups and downs of single
motherhood—happiness, fatigue, joy, guilt, worry, laughing
in good times, crying in bad times. The friendship lasted for
nearly a year.

In the sudden change that spurts from things that creep
up gradually, our friendship was strained when I bought a
house and moved from my apartment, and I changed my
career and had to work many more hours.

She lectured me about neglecting my child by working
so much and for being materialistic. I didn't think I
deserved that, nor did I think she was being fair, since her
own financial situation was deplorable. I felt this was
caused by her unwillingness to work at a "real" job, despite
the fact that neither of us receive reliable financial support
from our daughters' fathers.

Angrily, each not willing to confront the reality of her
own behavior, we stopped talking for the entire school year.
We'd smile in the elementary school hallways, but always
rush off to do something.

It hurt.

When I saw her, I noticed that her blond hair had longer and longer black roots—not just the kind that need a touch up, but inches and inches long. It looked awful. Her face became haggard, yet she was always the one volunteering to be the in-classroom aide for the teacher and to chaperone field trips. I marveled that she invested so much time at her daughter's school.

This heaped guilt on my busy shoulders, so I scurried back to my desk for another twelve-hour workday. I ate another chocolate chip cookie to help swallow my guilt and forget about my life and the fourteen extra pounds I'd gained by doing so.

I felt guilty for working. She felt guilty for not. Neither of us made a real move to reconcile. I missed my old friend and we'd send one another the occasional e-mail, but our affection was missing.

It was the classic guilt—working single mother feels bad about potential neglect. Stay-at-home single mother feels guilty for not working to provide a better life.

I was surprised when I realized we were both depressed, but for different reasons. Have you ever noticed it really is always darkest just before the dawn?

After years in court, Lizzy won a major legal battle and a gigantic check leapt into her life.

Meanwhile, my sixteenth book came out and for a brief fifteen minutes, I was as famous as I'd ever hoped to be.

I had crossed a major turning point in my life, and so had she. I saw her about two months ago, with all-the-way-blond hair, and it looked good. She had on makeup and wore a new shirt. But what looked even better was her radiant skin and big smile! She was back—and so was I. We'd both come through the "dark night of the soul" and emerged victorious, as those who persevere always do.

As if there had never been a breach, we picked up where we had left off. The girls are gleeful to be spending extra time together again.

When I look at my daughter's behavior, I see that she pays close attention to her friends. She knows their favorite colors and which songs they like best if they drive in the car with us after school. She can tell me what they like to eat, and which books they bought in the last book fair in third grade. When they fight, they make it up in a short while, a few days at the most, and no grudges seem to be borne for long.

How did I lose that skill? When did I stop caring that Lizzy was in so much pain that she was letting her roots turn black and was looking like an old woman? How did I not reach out during that time? Could it be that I was in so much pain I didn't see hers? Is that really an excuse to not love a friend?

Single mothers usually work. We often have a hard row to hoe. Building strong friendships is difficult with our intense schedules and exhausting routines. But how important those friendships are in the overall scheme of life! More than any other time in our lives, while we are single mothers we need the love and camaraderie of our girlfriends. Overlooking grievances and being big enough to forget grudges makes life much more pleasant and opens doors and hearts.

From now on, I'll watch Lizzy's hair. And tomorrow, I think I might even ask her what her favorite song is.

The Amazing Mrs. Kenna

When I was eleven years old, we moved to a rural new town in a new state far away from the life I'd known in a Chicago suburb. I hated it on sight. To make matters worse, my parents began attending a new church. It was a very small town, and I envisioned myself as a sophisticated city kid. There were very few kids my age at church. In fact, the only girl even close was a freckle-faced, scrawny, badly dressed girl with long stringy hair.

My mother is a meddlesome woman. She immediately spotted this waif-like kid and suggested I go introduce myself to this total stranger. I declined, so my beloved mama told me if I didn't go introduce myself I wouldn't be getting any dinner. I walked up to the girl, stuck out my hand to shake hers, and said something as pleasant as, "Hi. My name is Wendy Keller, and my mother said if I don't meet you, I can't have any dinner. What's your name?"

As it turned out, she was not only gracious enough to overlook my stupid introduction ("dorky" is what we would have called it then), but she became my best friend from about that moment forward. Most of the next twenty-five years of my life have included a lot of this dear soul. I spoke to her this morning, in fact.

Part of her amazing development comes from the example set by her mom, Tess Kenna. In the time I've known her, Mrs. Kenna has owned a flower shop and an upholstery shop and been an assessor for the county, taught classes at Northern Arizona State University, owned an appraisal company, bought and sold dozens of pieces of real estate, gone back to college and gotten not one but two degrees, one a Ph.D. in education, and almost single-handedly raised (get this!) *seven children!* Last time we spoke, she was starting an import business with two of her kids and a publishing company with another. By popular demand, AOL even voted her Queen for the day a while back!

Her ailing husband hasn't been able to be much help in the last few decades, so Mrs. Kenna has been a sort of single mother the whole time. She moved her enormous family to the remote city of Winslow, Arizona, bought a used *church*, nearly ten thousand square feet, and with her children, remodeled the whole thing!

Other than perhaps honorary membership in Overachievers Anonymous, Mrs. Kenna's other significant accomplishment is that her seven children love her. Every one of them is affectionate and comes home to visit. Every one of them went on to get a degree, and most of them hold highly successful jobs.

Mrs. Kenna isn't a typical mom in a lot of ways. She lives a much bigger than normal life, and has the energy of sixteen people. She sees only solutions where average people see problems. She uses her creativity, her ingenuity, and her drive to overpower, overcome, and overwhelm any obstacle that dares to raise its head. But her example reverberates through a community, through her children, through the lives of all who know her, myself included. What a dynamic legacy she is building! What a positive impact she has had on so many people.

Setting your mind to something has an amazing ability to catalyze the resources you need to finish the job. Mrs.

Kenna doesn't stop to wonder what to do if things go wrong—she knows they will sometimes, and she also knows she is prepared to overcome them when they do.

I for one want to raise an amazing child who grows up and loves me. I want to be a mother my child wants to hang out with on holidays. I want my daughter's friends to look back on the example I set once they are adults and say, "I learned a lot from that person." I want to be a mentor to others just by my example. I want to make a difference in this world while I'm here.

If you didn't have a Mrs. Kenna in your life to role model, why not become one yourself? Why not choose a half dozen goals today and start after them with all the energy, dynamism, and power you can muster? You may not finish everything, but chances are, you'll accomplish a lot more and feel greater self-esteem than if you do nothing but wish. By sheer willpower, the world moves aside and lets through the woman with the courage to claim what she wants in life.

Motivating the Troops

Whatever you do, do boldly. Boldness has a magic, a genius, a power in it. —Goethe, German philosopher

When my best friend and I were small, her dynamic mother, Mrs. Kenna, would welcome me like another one of her brood. I'd go home from church in Flagstaff with her family, enduring the three-hour ride back to their converted-church home in Winslow, Arizona. I'd stay a week or more and get a real chance to see how this woman operated. I didn't know it then, but in retrospect, she became one of my most important role models.

Mrs. Kenna made everything fun. She started grand projects. She dragged us all to charity events. She was always bustling with energy. She made meals big enough to feed hundreds of people, it seemed. She was completely unorthodox; she did things her own way at her own time. She dressed big, lived big, worked big. Her lipstick was too bright and her hair never perfectly combed. She always had a hundred hands in a thousand pies.

She canned food, she enlisted the children in cleaning the gigantic house, she helped out in the community, she started businesses that became profitable, and when she got bored, she started a new one. But at the same time, I can remember going to the laundry room, with its two washing machines she'd acquired on trade, and there were piles of clothes four feet thick on the floor, some of which had been wet for weeks. Their owners had outgrown some of them, while waiting for Mrs. Kenna to find time for them.

She set her own standards, and she kept them. When the youngest of her children was old enough, they all became involved in the local theater. When she got tired of it, she sold the flower shop she owned and began a new business. She was always moving, always talking.

After her daughter and I became adults, twenty years later, I arrived again at Mrs. Kenna's house—the same one she'd had when we were kids—with my one-year-old daughter for Lisa's wedding. We'd flown an hour, driven for four, and finally arrived at the church/house the Kennas homesteaded. After greeting me like her own kid, Mrs. Kenna and I set off with my baby into the basement room that the original pastor had used as a study. In front of us were acres and acres of white satin for Lisa's sumptuous wedding dress. Our job was to sew thousands of seed pearls onto it before the wedding the next day.

Mrs. Kenna pulled out two pieces of thread and two needles, and gave me a box of pearls. She chatted with me for probably five minutes. Once she'd set me well into the task, as was her style, she left me and my baby alone to go see to something. A hundred guests were on their way, and there was so very much to be done!

After she'd gone, I sat in the musty study sewing seed pearls onto my best friend's wedding dress and watching my baby nap beside me on a blanket. Perhaps an hour or more passed in the quiet while I sewed on seed pearls in the dwindling light, which gave me plenty of time to think. Among other things, I thought about how she managed to get me to sew on seed pearls for more than an hour.

When I tell someone to do something, a child, an employee, a coworker, I expect them to get themselves started and out of the sheer joy of following my always-logical order, I predict they will get involved in the task with as much force and determination as I would if I had time to do the job myself. I'm sure they will joyfully accomplish the task I give them, because my assignments are always terrific even if they aren't fun. I'm always surprised when something doesn't get done as fast or as precisely as I'd wished, or worse, when my worker simply gives up the task.

But Mrs. Kenna never does it that way. Every time she's talked someone into something, she always got nestled in, began it together with the poor sucker, chatted happily for a few moments, got the person really excited about whatever the person was supposed to be doing, whether it was making dinner, washing the floor, or sewing on darned seed pearls. Then she'd rush off to motivate the next person, accomplishing all her own tasks in a blur while she set everyone else to theirs.

I learned twenty bookfuls of things from the time I spent with Mrs. Kenna. She is hugely responsible for the woman I've become. But on this day in the basement, I saw a technique, a way of encouraging other people to do things they'd probably rather not do, which I have tried to use ever since. Whether it is my own child or a colleague, I find that when I use my own energy and enthusiasm to work with them at the start of a task, the momentum carries the other person through to completion. As long as I don't flit off irresponsibly, the helper finishes the task.

Just for the record, I sewed on seed pearls for nearly two hours before Mrs. Kenna came back to check on me. She took one look, announced, "Good job! Now come with me over here. I need some help with," and we were off on the next exciting adventure. Boy, oh, boy. If only I can get my kid to start vacuuming floors with the same enthusiasm!

Balancing Act

To soar on the heights of joy, we must first taste the bitter depths of sorrow. —Freidrich Neitzche, German philosopher

I go from stool to stool in singles bars hoping to get lucky, but there's never any gum under any of them.
—Emo Philips, comedian

I went to bed last night in one of the worst moods of the century. I hated everything—my life, my hopes, my dreams. I hated the effort it takes to be a mother. My daughter and I had had a major fight over homework again, and I was feeling exhausted by the stresses of single-handedly raising an eight-year-old who was everything my own mother had ever wished on me—my kid was just like me.

Life just didn't seem fair. My best friend had made a cruel comment, I'd watched the Gore-Bush debate and felt more confused than ever, and I let my daughter stay up too late afterward to play the video of *The Little Mermaid II*. Big mistake. She was overtired, I was overtired, the kitchen felt like wall-to-wall dishes, and I crawled into bed hoping tomorrow wouldn't come.

It came anyway.

To my great surprise, I woke up enthusiastic, grateful, and happy. I could handle another day. Heck, I could handle another week! Suddenly I felt encouraged and bright and energetic. It made me think about *balance*. When my life is out of balance, I feel wobbly. I feel out of stride, like I'm the one in the marching band whose feet are not moving in line with the rest.

I'm sure you've seen the circle of yin-yang, the Chinese symbol for life, balance, and equanimity. There are two swirls, one white with a black dot in the middle, one black with a white dot in the middle. Our lives are like that symbol. In the midst of the darkest side, there is always the white spot of hope. And in the midst of the white spot, there is always something that could be better.

In the midst of the darkest night, the dawn is coming. The promise of dawn is there. In the midst of the brightest day, most of us would think of improvements that would make things just a little bit better.

On the worst days of our lives, during the most stressed-out moments, it's fine to believe there's a white spot in our personal dark moment, but it doesn't help much unless you focus on it. I make myself focus on it, because like you, I cannot afford to be depressed. I pull out my diary and force myself to write five things I'm grateful for at that moment, and sometimes I add a little pep talk, reminding myself that good always returns in time. After all, at two in the morning, my diary is the easiest place to get a motivational injection.

Farmers have a grip on life's cycles and seasons because they notice the planet going through her cycles. After a bountiful fall harvest comes the harsh winter, followed by the bright spring, dawn of new hope. A spider dies after laying her egg sack, but babies are born after her death. Life has cycles, days have cycles, and people have cycles too.

If you take a broad view of your life, you will see your own cycles. The physical cycles of your body, the cycle of childbearing, and the sleep-wake cycles are all part of our existence. Some days, I think I can break the cycles of my life. I think if I work just a little harder or clean just one more thing, somehow I'll be able to "get ahead" and break the up and down cycle that is life. I'm not so sure I can. In my life, and probably in yours too, the cycles just keep spiraling through the days of our lives.

If I look at my life as an amorphous swirling mist of the yin-yang symbol, I see that there are good times and bad. There's always up and down, and as sure as I go into one phase, I will eventually go into the corresponding other. Nobody can be on the top of the mountain all the time, and even if she could be, would it bring the joy she hopes for?

Think of the world as a big circle, a ball in space. If you are standing in your house and someone else is standing in her house in Africa and another woman is doing the same in China, who is on top? If it's a circle, where is the top? Can you ever be on top of everything?

I believe that accepting the cycles of our lives, the good and the bad, makes it easier to take both what's easy and what's difficult in stride. It helps us accept the open times and the closed times. If I had had the wisdom to consciously observe my bad attitude before I went to bed last night, I would have been able to write in my diary and remind myself that tomorrow would necessarily be better, as the earth and all its cycles strive for balance.

Today, I will look at my life from a broader perspective than the moment I am in. When I hear myself talking too fast, I will speak slower. When I see myself getting angry at slow drivers when I am late on my way to pick up my child after school, I will send good wishes to every person who gets in my way. When I find myself walking too slowly, I will speed up. When I find myself awake but exhausted, I will rest. In this way, I will help balance my life, and I will teach myself to accept the larger ups and downs that occur in everyday existence. Exploring both sides will help me find my own middle.

Givers Gain

*When fate's got it in for you, there's no limit to what
you may have to put up with.*
—Georgette Heyer, *English novelist*

It was almost 3 A.M. on Saturday two weeks before Christmas.
Martin and Susan were not only up, they were on the road
after only a few hours' sleep. Not your typical do-gooders,
they had volunteered this morning to join a group of others
to distribute donated food and toys to indigent inner-city
families. They expected to work the whole twelve hours of
the mission, maybe longer.

His son and her daughter were away for the weekend at
the other parents'. He grabbed a cup of coffee, and in the
bleary-eyed predawn, they climbed into Martin's car. The
loading station for the food bank was miles away, and to get
there, they had to drive twenty minutes through a winding
canyon before turning onto the main highway. At this time
of morning the roads were clear. The drunks were already
crashed somewhere, and the early workers were still asleep.
They drove in drowsy silence.

About halfway through the twisting canyon road, Martin
suddenly slammed on the brakes. A few feet ahead, a gigantic boulder as big as a car had fallen from the cliff above and
landed in the middle of both lanes. Pausing to catch their
breath and exclaim at the size of the rock, they inched
around it in the darkness and continued on their way.

Once their cell phone had a clear signal, they reported
the boulder to the highway patrol and made it safely to

their destination. In the hullabaloo of packaging dry foods, canned goods, and fresh fruits and vegetables, they forgot about the boulder. When the teams of hundreds of people from all over the county met to deliver the packages, the joy on the faces of the recipients evaporated all thoughts of their own brush with death.

Sometimes, bad things happen to good people. Everyone knows that. But often good things happen to good people, too. Although it may be a stretch to suggest that Martin was able to stop the car as a benefit of the good mission they were on, and it is unlikely that his reflexes would have been slower if they had merely been out for their own pleasure, the truth is, this happened.

There are plenty of ways to test the concept. The results might not come immediately, and then again, they might. Try today to out-give the Universe. Be nicer, sweeter, gentler, more patient than ever before. When you have to deal with an angry customer, coworker, or client, go the extra mile to reassure them that you and your company really care about their satisfaction. When someone cuts you off on the road, don't shake your fist or mutter things about where they may have learned to drive. Smile through your gritted teeth and wish them well. When your child gets whiny, be the strong one today—don't go there. See if maybe, just maybe, changing your position doesn't change the world.

Teetering on the Totter

I believe the lasting revolution comes from deep changes in ourselves which influence our collective life. —Anais Nin, *author*

Men read maps better than women because only men can understand the concept of an inch equaling a hundred miles. —Roseann Barr, *comedian*

Balance. Balance is what happens when two people weigh the same amount, and both sit on a teeter-totter at the same time. It is what happens when people who are equal or circumstances that are equal balance one another out. How do we create balance in our lives? By applying consciousness to the words and actions we take. We can achieve balance with our children by remembering that an overly hard response from us brings the same from them, and that a soft answer turns away wrath. There are many opportunities in a day to bring balance into our lives.

There are unending opportunities to achieve a more peaceful balance in our lives if we will only learn the laws, the principles, the ways of bringing balance into our lives. But when things are in perfect balance, which they rarely are, they do not move. Theoretically, both bodies would dangle in midair on the teeter-totter, the scales would settle perfectly. Life moves as long as we're alive; we never reach The Destination until we're dead. While greater balance helps us feel centered, perfect balance is not only impossible, but also undesirable.

I feel most out of balance when I have been struggling with something. It reminds me of the saying "Let go and let God," which implies that we should do the best we can and allow God to do the rest. When I was a child in parochial high school, there was a sign on the classroom wall above my desk. It said: "Act as if it all depends on you, live as if it all depends on God." I think that locked within this statement, representative of a tradition of faith, is a secret that mothers can use to balance their lives. It is a secret we can use to create a loving sense of equanimity in our relationships with our children, our environment, our coworkers, and ourselves.

Have you ever noticed that when you get angry with someone or something, everything you see becomes negative? That's because, in that moment, you are focusing on what's bad about the person or situation, so everything becomes dark. Try this experiment now: Look around the room you are in. Quickly count the number of objects in the room that are blue. Go ahead, do it right now. How many items are blue? The color of the sky, the color of water, dark blue, light blue; just count everything that is blue! Now shut your eyes.

Take a deep breath, and keep your eyes closed. Now, without opening your eyes, tell me how many objects in the room are *black*. That's right. How many things are black? If you are in a room you know, it may not be that hard to determine a number. But you weren't looking for black when I told you to look for blue, were you? No, you saw what you were looking for. You saw exactly what you were looking for. Open your eyes and see how many things are black. Now count how many things are red, or green, or some other color (or shape or material). This experiment is equally true in life. We each see precisely what we are looking for. If you go through life looking for sky-blue things, you will certainly find them. If you go through life looking for dark, black things, you will find those instead.

How you live your life is a choice. You can choose to see yourself as a victim, and you'll become one. No one can convince you that you are not, darn it. Or you can choose to see yourself as the organized, loving mother that you are, confident in a bright day today and a brighter one tomorrow. Take responsibility for your life where you are now, and transform your vision of who you are and where you are going. The choice is yours, and it's as simple as choosing where you will focus.

Starry Eyes

Reach high, for stars lie hidden in your soul. Dream deep, for every dream precedes the goal. —Pamela Vaull Starr, renowned foster mother, author

The quality of a person's life is in direct proportion to their commitment to excellence, regardless of their chosen field of endeavor. —Vince Lombardi, football coach

Sometimes, hoping is so fervent it prevents us from doing. Lucinda lives in LA. She is pretty, not beautiful. She is smart, not brilliant. She is kind and soft, not bold and commanding. She is effective, but not energetic. At forty-three years old, she was still waiting to be discovered.

I accept the fact that I live in LA and, therefore, every third person I see is someone waiting to be discovered by the Hollywood studios and be turned into a major actor. These people fuel themselves and each other with stories of the one person, a friend of a friend's friend, who out of six million people was actually discovered sitting in a coffee shop next to a producer or something.

The Bible says, "Hope deferred makes the heart sick," and this was true for Lucinda. She had become almost nuts about this being discovered thing. She always thought about it, she always talked about it. She went to countless auditions, taking unpaid time off from a paying job she hated to pursue her dream of becoming a starlet.

At first, I wondered how she could justify following her dream so intensely. I thought it was more than a little impractical. She was obsessed with becoming a famous actor. When confronted about this obsession, she would defiantly say, "Someday, I'll give up on this if I don't make it. But I'm not ready to yet," and she'd rush off to another audition.

She still goes to auditions, and she even does a few commercials. It's been two years since I met her, and I don't think she's going to turn into a famous starlet. It's too bad, because we'd all like this story to have a happy ending. We'd all like me to write "and then she was discovered and lived happily ever after on the big screen." But that isn't what happened. And Lucinda is negative now, beaten down and sad and bitter. She feels like she sacrificed a lot of her self-worth auditioning for hundreds of people who didn't want her in the end.

Success in life or with something during our life has four ingredients. First, we must decide what we want. Second, we must take steps to get it—take action—move in that direction. Third, we must check our progress every so often, just like our kids get report cards, to see if we're getting closer to our destination or goal, or not. And fourth, and perhaps most important, we must adjust accordingly. Kids get tutors when their midterm report cards say they are failing in math. That's an adjustment. Adults get financial counseling, or find a new job, or change their strategy when they are having problems with work. But not Lucinda. She skipped steps three and four, and as a result, she is nowhere near her goal, and she's sad.

Wanda is at the other end of the spectrum. She is also living in LA waiting to be discovered. The castoff wife of a big CEO who dumped her for the proverbial secretary,

Wanda slumped when her man left. Forsaken to raise an obstreperous son, a rebellious teenage daughter, and eleven-year-old twins, with only the occasional help of their father, Wanda sunk into a black depression for years after her divorce.

Single motherhood wasn't working well for her. Single motherhood was more trouble than she could stand. She was depressed, alone, and couldn't understand how the man she "had done everything for" could possibly have left.

She floated in the warm memories of the glory days of her life. She'd been an actress in a soap opera when Mr. Wonderful had swept her off her feet. She'd left her dreams behind and dedicated her life to him and their four ungrateful children. And now what did she have?

She had a house in a great neighborhood, a guilt present from the ex. She had enough money every month to live comfortably. She had all the children she wanted and didn't want more. She was pretty, petite, and funny. She had a lot of charm, and her years as one of the social elite made her comfortable in many settings. She had a lot more going for her than she was willing to recognize those first years.

I see many women who focus mostly on what they don't have anymore. Wanda did that for a while. Then she abruptly realized that her life wasn't over.

She started working. She got a job at a comedy club doing standup, and she was successful! She auditioned for a few parts, and she got them! She applied for a few modeling jobs, and she got several of those, too. Eventually, as she kept at it, she created her own act, a dream she'd had as a young woman. Now she lives comfortably on her own money, money she earns from doing work she loves.

She bolstered her self-esteem, and when she did, her children began to treat her with respect. They stopped seeing Mom as everyone's doormat and started seeing the woman she was becoming.

There's an expression: "Shoot for the moon, and you might just catch a few stars." Both of these women once wanted to be famous. But Wanda converted her dream into being happy, truly happy, with a handful of stars. As a result, she has achieved more peace of mind, personal success, and self-esteem than Lucinda, who believes if you don't get precisely what you want, it proves you're a loser. I think I'd rather be like Wanda.

Penelope and the Guilt-O-Meter

*The neighborhood children didn't have to take naps, and we'd
lean out the window talking to them until we were found out,
and then we were supposed to go back to bed and rest.*
—Adele Kanaley Miller Christensen,
"My Mother Before Me"

Dr. Penelope Leach writes parenting books. *Your Baby and
Child from Birth to Age Five* is probably her most renowned
work—you might have a copy on your shelf. Parents have
always relied on "experts" to guide them on raising their
child. When many of us were children, our parents read Dr.
Spock's book on child rearing. Perhaps you can remember
the day Dr. Spock's words of wisdom changed your life. I
dreaded it whenever my parents "discovered" some new
parenting author, but at least a book didn't carry as much
clout as a real live lecture!

When I was about eleven, our church got a new minister. He had gray hair and wore thick black-rimmed
glasses, and he wore very solid, dependable shoes. He
decided that the parents in his congregation needed lots of
information on parenting. Little devils that we were, I
suppose he could have been right. So he began lecturing.
My parents and my friends' parents listened.

Every time he gave a sermon on parenting, we knew we
were in for a week of hell. We knew our parents would try

incredibly hard on Monday to implement precisely what Mr. Foster said. On Tuesday, they would still be trying hard, and our lives would still be miserable. By Wednesday, they would still be trying. On Thursday, they would be trying to remember the rules they'd made on Sunday afternoon, and by Friday, things would be pretty much back to normal. Whew!

I'd see my friends at church and we'd commiserate about the rough week we'd had, and we'd pray that Mr. Foster would talk about something that didn't involve child rearing, like "the fruits of the spirit" or "Christian service" or something. Then we'd be free to be normal kids until the next sermon.

Now that I'm a mom, I admit that when I am overwhelmed, I read parenting books at 2 A.M. I read them because there's no one to talk to about how I'm raising my child except maybe my girlfriends who are also single parents, and they won't love me if I call them at 2 A.M.

Every time I read a book, including Penelope's, I think about all the things I'm doing wrong. I think about how desperately I want to do everything right. I vow I'll make big changes, and sometimes I do. I've been known to tack new lists overnight to the refrigerator, just like an elf at Christmas. I've been known to use cash rewards to try to motivate a child who still cannot tell the monetary difference between a dime (which is small) and a penny (which is bigger and prettier to look at).

But what I know, and what my child knows, and what I venture to guess you and your child(ren) know, is that for the most part, it's a temporary change. Just like when I was a kid dreading the week after a parenting sermon, I knew that if I could just endure the new rules long enough, the sermon would wear off and my parents would return to normal.

What I didn't know when I was a kid was that my parents felt guilty about going back to being normal. I didn't know until I told my own mother I felt guilty when my stringent reforms of domestic policy faded away after just a few days or a week. She admitted she'd felt the same.

I asked around. Almost every parent I spoke to told me stories of their own guilt. They told me about feeling guilty when they didn't spend enough time with their kid, or when they yelled last week, or how they always have bad mornings before school, or how they hate helping the kid with homework, or how they apply and then fail to enforce a new rule, or how they wonder about this or worry about that.

In the process of this informal research, I realized something. It's the good parents who worry—it's the good parents who occasionally feel a bit guilty. I subscribe to an adage that helps me deal with parenting guilt: The definition of good parenting is raising a child who can afford to pay for his or her own therapy.

Although I'm guessing this is meant as a joke, in some ways it's true. You know you're trying your best. Maybe raising a child, worrying about whether you are doing it right, thinking about your parenting decisions, and trying to be consistent *is* good parenting. It's possible that the love you express by constantly trying, by always caring, by always loving and learning more, maybe, just maybe, that is what makes you a good mom.

Am I Doing This Right?

I got kicked out of ballet class because I pulled a groin muscle, even though it wasn't mine. —Gilda Radner, comedian

In my down moments, I sometimes suspect that I am making some egregious mistake that will forever damage my child. Worse, I do not even know what that mistake might be! Will she remember a harsh word spoken the time I was sick and tired and she was whining? Will it be how I made her eat foods I thought were healthy and deprived her of candy before dinner? Or will it be something more serious? How about the time she caught me kissing a new boyfriend when I thought she was downstairs? Will it be the fact that I share more of my life and feelings with her than I would if I had a mate to share some of them with?

To make matters worse, every now and then some stupid study comes out that deplores all of us divorced parents—millions of us—and says that our children are at significantly higher risk for all sorts of problems, from academic to social, through their entire life. Ours are the kids who will flunk out, do drugs, get pregnant in high school, crash their own marriages more frequently, and so on.

Then, a few months later, another study comes out that says the original study was wrong because it was based on warped data and incorrect representative population samples. Argh! If you're like me all this confuses you. I throw up my hands, resolve to do the best I can, come what may. There's little I can do to change the past.

47

At the coffee shop this morning, I ran into Beverly. Her son is in law school now, and there couldn't be a prouder mom. She raised her son alone—her entire life. She made the same sacrifices and had the same concerns we all do about our children.

Bev sits across the coffee table from me and shoves a tired hand through her short blond curls. "Now that my son is in college, I have all this free time," she laments, saddened by the empty nest. "I always thought it would be so great, but now I really miss him." She tells me how she would have chosen a different career had she not had a child to raise. She tells me how she would have lived her life differently if she had known then what she knows now. I want to know what she knows.

Bev tells me how she sacrificed her life for her son—how she worked and slaved, cooked dinner, cleaned the house, did the homework, built a tiny business on the side, scrimped and saved, and didn't have time to date or really even live while she was raising him. She told me that a fear of failure drove her to make choices that she wouldn't have made if the risk had been only her own.

She regrets not having taken more risks, she says now. "I'd have taken more risks professionally, personally, romantically, emotionally, financially, you know. I'd have lived a bigger life."

It got me thinking. How many times do I make choices based on my child's well-being that somewhere down the line I may regret? The choices that seem the best at the time—are they really the best choices in the long term?

"I still worry about him," Bev tells me. "Did I do the right things? I'm proud of the man he's become, but I spent his childhood wondering whether I was doing it right. As he grows, I feel more gratified that I did well, but it's still scary. We want so much for our children, and as single parents we invest so heavily in them, more than we would if we had another relationship—a marriage—to also invest in."

Bev sits back in her chair and stares out the window for a second. I see the light on her middle-aged face, and I know she has been a good mother. Around town, people know her child as a good and honest young man. She did well. But did she somehow lose herself in the process?

It's easy to mistake our child as our confidant when we are single parents. We tell them things about our dating life that a child raised in an intact home wouldn't hear. We expose them to feelings like fatigue, boredom, or a bad day at work, that a married parent would share with a spouse, not a child. We perhaps burden them too early with our adult cares.

Some of us single moms go to the other extreme and create perennial juveniles of our children by working ourselves to death to make it easy and comfortable for them. Out of our guilt, we do all the household chores and readily give up every luxury, every nice thing for ourselves, to spend more money on our child. This way, we become emotional throw rugs and invite our children and others to walk all over us. Later, we'll feel justified in acting the martyr. Sadly, martyrs are rarely beloved.

Both extremes would seem to create children who are maladjusted in the world, don't you think? The harsh reality of parenting is that you are raising this child to leave you, live long, prosper, and be happy. You are not in a permanent living-together relationship, and there will come a day, whether through the child's own impetus or society's, that he or she will grow up and leave you. That's as it should be.

Will your child leave you as an empty shell with no place to go and no personal interests outside parenting? Someone who forgot to look interesting to other adults, who gained all that extra weight because she didn't care, who forgot to read good books or take up interesting hobbies or classes?

What kind of a parent will you be when your child is ready to leave you for college or work or a love of their own? Will you have such an empty life that you entreat her to stay? Or will you hold open the front door for her on her way out, welcoming her back if need be, but encouraging her growth and maturity in the years to come?

Green Rivers of Cash

No one would remember the Good Samaritan if he only had good intentions. He had money as well. —Margaret Thatcher, former Prime Minister of Great Britain

I don't know much about being a millionaire, but I'll bet I'd be darling at it. —Dorothy Parker, celebrity

At the mall today, I noticed a large number of grand cars parked in a row. I passed several Mercedes and Lexuses and Range Rovers and other expensive luxury cars all lined up, their owners inside shopping.

It reminded me of something a car salesman told me, "Most people lease the most expensive car they can possibly afford. They end up with gigantic payments, and we end up with huge profits. I'd always rather lease a car to someone with a big ego than sell a used car to someone frugal—the commissions are larger and the negotiation is easier."

At lunch with Vikki, a mid-thirties single mom who works for a bank, we talk about the financial risks of being the lone provider and how truly that affects the single parent, no matter how much money they make. The fear of not having enough money someday, today or last week, haunts most of us, I've found, no matter what our income level. There's always the risk of losing everything, of not being able to make ends meet. As my mom used to say, "Just about the time you think you can make ends meet, somebody moves the ends!"

Most of the single moms I informally polled said that making and keeping money is one of their biggest concerns about single parenting.

"What if I get sick?"

"How can I put anything away for college? I don't even have enough to live on!"

"There are always more bills than money!"

"Retirement! That's a laugh. I'll be lucky to get through this year."

These complaints are compounded in some cases by deadbeat dads who can't or simply don't pay child support, or by men who take no real responsibility for the extras their children need—lessons, braces, health care. Stephanie, a thirty-seven-year-old single mother, makes it work on her own, like so many of us do. Her ex-husband had to file bankruptcy, and he changes jobs frequently. There's rarely a steady check coming in, no matter what the court requires.

This is not a book on managing your finances, and I am not the poster child for fiscal wellness, although I'm learning. But the subject fascinates me because I do have complete responsibility for my child's fiscal well-being.

I know that I live in a culture where people always want more. If my child has to have brand-name tennis shoes, it might mean we have to do without something else. The great motivational speakers may proudly claim that the amount of money you have is determined only by your attitude, and they may be right, but in the meantime, most people spend at least as much money as they can imagine

52

earning, and more. This can gnaw at the pit of your stomach and diverts emotional and intellectual resources that could provide security. The Dalai Lama, in his excellent book, *The Art of Happiness*, written with Howard Cutler says, "Ask yourself if this will give you pleasure or happiness." Pleasure is fleeting and often expensive.

Our individual consumer credit debt is terrifying, and many Americans live a half step ahead of the creditors—and you know how vicious they can be! One single man I dated told me, "If I ever meet a woman who doesn't know the brand of another woman's purse and has no credit card debt, I'll marry her on the spot!" I didn't fit his criteria.

There seems to be a basic preoccupation with what we need now and what we want now. People buy what they want, not always what they need. For instance, a fifteen-ounce bag of corn chips is about the same price as a couple of pounds of fruit. Fruit is healthier, fruit is more filling, and fruit probably will hang out in your kitchen longer, but corn chips taste better, so we buy them.

Like the car salesman says, a lot of purchases are bought for ego's sake. We want to look good, smell good, live good, feel good, and look wealthier than we actually are, and we want our children to do the same. We want to project an image that everything is okay and we're doing great. It makes us feel better to drive a leased, expensive car than a paid-for wreck.

One of the most life-affirming things we can do as single mothers is to stop overspending. Stop putting money on credit cards, and pay them off! Imagine your money is like the water in a pitcher. There's only so much in it before it needs to be replenished.

Put just $20 per paycheck into an envelope, or $100 or $50—whatever you can afford. It's the old adage "Pay yourself first." Keep the money in your house, and let it be your little secret—don't tell your kids it is there. And don't use it. Let it be the spring from which your cash river begins to flow.

Now you can pour some water out of the pitcher. Much of it will pay for utility bills and your rent or mortgage, of course. But everything else, and I mean every remaining expense, can be reduced temporarily while you dig yourself out of the hole and get yourself financially well again. Won't that feel incredible?

On clothing, for example, do you really need that sweater, even though it's on sale? How many garments can you wear at one time? Pioneer women often had two work dresses and maybe one for church. They wore one work dress while washing the other! Do you need another pair of shoes? Will the pleasure really be worth the bill at the end of next month?

I found my tendency is to give in when my kid asks for something. I am not sure whether I do this out of guilt or just because I am a lenient person by nature, but even if she already has a new box of crayons, I'll say yes to one more box or to a book at the bookstore since I brought her there anyway. I'll buy one more pair of jeans—after all, it's just an easy slide of the credit card. In a few weeks, I've spent $30 or more that I didn't really think about at the time.

You don't need to spend much money on prepackaged foods. You can make school lunches for the kids, and you can carry lunch to work for a few months or so. An Oscar Meyer Lunchable® for your kid every day will cost you more than $10 a week, and if you add morning coffee for yourself, you might be spending $50 or more per month that you really don't need to.

I agree that you cannot completely give up luxuries, and I hate the thought of economizing as much as the next person. I still splurge on one "luxury" item when I am going through a "get my finances back in order" period in my life. For me (don't laugh!), it is soap. I will continue to buy and use really nice soap. But I will ruthlessly cut out anything else to pay off those debts. It's odd, but I actually enjoy the soap more during thrifty times.

In some ways, I am lucky to come from an extremely frugal family. I know where to cut corners, even if I don't want to. Simple things like using cloth napkins and real plates, not plastic ones, save a few bucks. Buying a frozen pizza to have on hand in an emergency instead of calling for delivery saves you $20 plus a tip. It may not seem like the little things matter, but $20 here and $40 there pretty soon add up to an extra $100 a month to pay down the credit card. And once the credit card is paid off, just look at all the real money you'll have—no more interest payments on things you cannot even remember buying! It's like giving yourself a raise, and you don't even have to ask for it.

Mrs. Potash, The Martyr of Maryland

I never understood the fear of some parents about babies getting mixed up at the hospital. What difference does it make as long as you get a good one?
—Heywood Broun, journalist

When my children become wild and unruly, I use a nice, safe playpen. When they're finished, I climb out.
—Erma Bombeck, comedian

I have a friend whose mother was a bitter, unpleasant woman when we were kids. Mrs. Potash was always harping on something, because nothing was ever good enough, never fully right. Her mission in life was to keep the house and her three kids perfectly neat. In order to accomplish this, Mrs. Potash spent a lot of time talking to her children about all the things she could have done and could have been had she not chosen to become a mother at age twenty-two. By her reasoning, this meant that my friend and her siblings were now obligated to help their mother stop suffering by cleaning up their rooms and helping sweep the kitchen floor without being asked.

That woman spent her whole life being involved with her children, always saying that next year, when one got in school, or when they all got in school or when they all got in full-time school, or when they all got out of high school, or when they all got out of college, then she would finally live her life for herself. Mrs. Potash drove herself, her husband, and her children crazy.

My friend, the youngest child, has been out of the house for eleven years now, and if you speak with Mrs. Potash now, she'll talk about all the things she plans to do after her husband finally retires! She is still a martyr to her fictitious captors. But they're all gone and prefer not to visit.

I don't want to live my life that way. I don't want my child to grow up in the household of a martyr. I don't want my world to be full of "somedays." I want to show my child an example of a healthy, happy, productive, well-adjusted mother now, not someday.

There are only so many hours in a life. What if we spend them wishing, not living our lives? I left my marriage partly to set an example for my child of not staying in a toxic situation. Should I now live in the pain and trauma of not living my dreams because I'm waiting for someday, when my kid is gone? Wouldn't that make me resentful and make her feel like she didn't ask to be born?

Mrs. Potash's daughter, my friend, has a deep sense of not belonging, not really being wanted. Not only does it affect her, it affects how she parents her kids. She sees her own children as occasional impediments to her life, not always as blessings along the path. It's what she learned as a child. I know she fights against it bitterly, but the pattern is long ingrained.

Where there's a will there's a way, they always say. I'm reminded of women who overcame great odds, with or without children, to achieve their dreams and improve the quality of their lives and their children's lives. I know stories of bold women who struggled and lived victoriously despite whatever stood in their way.

It's hard to imagine why anyone would spend his or her life waiting to start living, isn't it? It's nearly a mortal sin if we wait for someone else to give us permission to live. I suspect it's secretly an excuse for not having the courage to try, lest we fail. But without trying, we leave a life of little meaning behind when we die.

I resolve to dream, and dream big. To ask myself, "How can I make this work for all of us?" as opposed to focusing daily on why things aren't as I wish they could be. Motherhood, parenthood, is a sacred responsibility, and we cannot shirk it except to the detriment of our own children, their peers and their generation, and ultimately their planet. But life is for living, and when we are brave enough to dream, we are ready to soar!

The Power of One

We had a quicksand box in the backyard. I was an only child,
eventually. —Emo Phillips, comedian

Ask your child what he wants for dinner only if he's buying.
—Fran Lebowitz, writer

I admit that I worry sometimes. I worry that my daughter
will turn into a monster when she turns twelve and discov-
ers hormones. I worry that somebody else's kid will influence her into using some drug, or doing something she'll
regret for the rest of her life. I worry that she'll see something in a movie that contaminates her mind from seeing
the beauty and sanctity of making love.

I have been known to worry that she'll feel cheated
because she came from "a broken home," although how it
is more broken now than it was when I was married evades
me. I wonder whether she'll miss it when her father doesn't
show up for open house even with a desire to come because
he lives an hour a way and has a job and another family and
that this will effect her expectations of men.

I learned something, though, that I pull out of my
mental file and read to myself when I'm in a Worried Mom
state. (This usually occurs two days before my period at
approximately 2 A.M.) I learned the power of example, the
Power of One. I am the one with the power to influence her
destiny. I am the one who is with her most of the time. I am
the one who has to show her what I stand for. I am the one
who must teach her my perspective on everything from

morality to how to eat gracefully with a soupspoon. ("Just as a ship goes out to sea," I rejoinder at the dinner table, "I dip my spoon away from me!")

There's only one person I can truly take responsibility for, mind, body and soul. It isn't my child. It is me. I'm the one who can optimistically toss out a bunch of adages, or the one who can fail as parent by insisting, "Do as I say, not as I do." I'm only truly in charge of myself, and the responsibility I have for my child, in theory, diminishes year by year as she nears adulthood.

After all, the goal is to raise a young woman who can think for herself, knows right from wrong, and can become a profitable, happy member of society.

If this is true, then I will teach more from my *example* than I ever will from my edicts. Saying, "You simply must finish your homework right now!" and then turning in my own project late is inconsistent. Discussing the value I place on her education the morning she'd much prefer to play hooky loses a lot of impact if I use sick days to skip my own work, or if I drop her off tardy in the schoolyard each morning.

I believe in goals, as you, dear reader, will surely have seen by now in this book. So I listed the character traits I think are most honorable in another. I listed those qualities I find true in my dearest friends, in my own mother, in women I admire in the media and in public service. I listed the traits I would deeply respect in a woman. Obviously, this would work with boys, too, if one listed the traits of the ideal man.

Then, working backward, I thought about how I would like to see these traits in my daughter. I'd like her to be a better woman than I am in every way. But the only way she's going to get there is if I blaze the trail. Against this list of ideal traits, I measure my own character, my own deeds, my own speech. I measure the things I say to myself, and evaluate how close I am to my ideal.

I know that to instill these traits in my daughter will take conscious, concerted effort, both to model them and to teach them. Like the proper use of the soupspoon with its little ditty that I didn't learn until I was fifteen, I want her to be gracious, poised, compassionate, eloquent, learned, giving, elegant, joyful, and so many other things.

We often worry about how our children will turn out, when perhaps we would be wiser to modify how we've turned out, and make the appropriate changes to ourselves. Remember the wonderful poem "Children Learn What They Live"? If a child lives with criticism, it will learn to be critical and so on.

Our children, we know, will take more from our example and less from our words than we'd like. Will they model our best behavior, or will they mimic the things we wished they had not noticed? Thinking back to my own parents, I notice that when I am under stress I immediately do what my mother would have done in that situation, even though I have not lived with her for more than twenty years! Perhaps you notice similarly automatic responses in yourself, or you see other patterns you picked up that are not consistent with the ideal person you would like your child to become.

If I pretend I mirror to my child the woman she will someday be, I am much more likely to act in a manner consistent with my goals for her life. I also know that by using the power I have over myself, I am using the Power of One to overcome negative influences from the outside. I don't want her to obey me when she is a teen "because I said so." I want her to live a life of integrity and beauty because that is who she has become.

When we ponder our example and the Power of One, we see that the shackles of worry are broken, and our hearts and spirits are free to soar with the loftiest goals we have for our beloved children.

Single Dads

My father was frightened of his father, I was frightened of my father, and I am damned well going to see to it that my children are frightened of me.
—George V, former King of England

The highlight of my childhood was making my brother laugh so hard that food came out his nose. —Garrison Keillor, author

Sometimes, because there are more of us, I make the mistake of thinking that it is only single mothers who raise children alone in this world.

At my daughter's elementary school, there are only a dozen or so single dads. I spoke to one of them, George, who is also raising a daughter. Her mother crumbled from substance abuse, and they couldn't make it work any more. He's got 99 percent custody, and she's got supervised visitation.

I asked him what it's like being a single dad. He said there are so few other men who are also single dads that parents of other little girls are wary. Many of them feel so uncomfortable they won't allow their daughters to play at his house because they assume he's a pervert of some sort. He reports that there are many mothers who won't allow their daughters to have sleepovers at his house. He said it's difficult to imagine the prejudice he feels. Single parents are still relatively rare, and single dads are not only rare, but are subject to suspicion. I think that being a single dad may be even more difficult than being a single mom.

When I speak to the few single dads I know well, I ask them what their experience of parenting is like. What always surprises me is that they have the same concerns, worries, pain, guilt, joy, and delight that we moms have in our children. In fact, in my limited experience, it seems like single dads are every bit as committed to their child(ren) as single moms are.

Yet as a mother with a little girl, I wouldn't casually allow my child to spend the night at a friend's house, either, especially if the dad was single. I tell George this, and he agrees. But then he asks, "Wouldn't you do the same if she were going to sleep over at a married parents' house? Isn't that dad as likely or unlikely to be a pervert as some mothers seem to accuse me of being?"

I had to think about that. "How would you suggest people get around this?" I ask. "You know it will continue to come up throughout your daughter's life."

He nods his head sadly. "I suggest that we meet in public places, like parks or amusement parks or restaurants for kids. I offer that we all go together. I meet the moms and try to talk with them. Some are open to that; others think I'm trying to seduce them out of their marriages. It's not true, of course. It's a lonely life because there are so few men who are committed to raising their children alone in our society."

George's ex-wife is not available emotionally to provide for their daughter's social needs. It's the kids that suffer in this case. Bruce, another single dad in his mid-forties, told me, "My son was excluded from his playmates because the moms got together and did their kid thing together. A lot of times they would make plans, and he wouldn't get to go. It makes your kid feel like he's not accepted, like he's not part of the group. It made him feel more needy and created a self-esteem issue for John that makes me feel bad."

I joined a single-parents group a few years back, sponsored by my child's school. There were, of course, a lot of single moms there. There were a half-dozen single dads. A few of the single dads had only alternate weekend custody, and they were obviously there looking for a woman who could help them out when they got stuck with their kid for the weekend, not for help with their parenting issues.

But the other single dads really broke my heart as they described being ostracized from talking about child rearing and homework issues, discipline, and the school play. "I'm the only real parent my daughter has," George said. "And I feel all alone sometimes because I didn't grow up learning how to do this. I had to learn everything the hard way, and there's almost no woman brave enough to talk to me without thinking that I'm trying to make it into something sexual."

I think the next time I see a single dad sitting alone at the park, I'll strike up a conversation. It won't be in hopes of meeting Mr. Right or with the illusion that he molests all little kids except his own. It will be in hopes of making a new friend and perhaps reaching out to a person in need.

For the Love of Money

I had plastic surgery last week. I cut up my credit cards.
—Henny Youngman, comedian

I could now afford all the things I didn't have as a kid, if I didn't have kids. —Robert Orben, comedy writer

Fun is about making memories with your kids, memories that will last a lifetime. But fun hasn't got anything to do with money. If you don't believe it, go to expensive Disneyland. There are plenty of people there having a simply awful time.

Not being able to provide your children with expensive trips, clothes, and other things doesn't necessarily make you a good or bad parent. It's all in how you handle it. One mother I know couldn't even afford proper dressers for her children's clothes. All three of the children kept their clothes in neatly folded stacks on the floor until this mother came up with a brilliant idea.

She took her three children to the grocery store and told each child to pick out two rolls of their favorite contact paper. After they'd bought the contact paper for a few dollars a roll, she drove around back where the store stacked the cardboard boxes it had used.

The family went home and together covered the boxes with contact paper, in each child's favorite color, and stacked them in the corners of their bedroom to make festive and bright and useful "dressers."

Now this story shows ingenuity on the mother's part and a high degree of resourcefulness. But the mother didn't tell this story to me. It was told to me by the oldest daughter, who nearly thirty years later still remembers this as one of the warmest memories of her childhood. She remembers it as fun!

The mother, were she still alive, might not remember that particular event as fun. She might look back on that time in her life with sadness because she wasn't able to provide her children with the things other mothers could.

I found that story heartwarming in the extreme, a real tribute to this mother's inventiveness. I asked for more.

My friend said that a few years later, when all three children were in their early teens, their mother was able to trade some clerical services for a small rowboat. The boat was dilapidated, the once-white marine paint peeling from the sides, and one seat unsafe to sit on, but the hull was sound.

The mother turned this boat into a family project. For the next few months of weekends, they stripped it, sanded it, rebuilt the seat, found oars at a garage sale, and painted the boat.

The family tugged that boat behind their beat-up old Chevrolet every weekend all through summer vacations, holidays, and sometimes after school. Parked in the front yard, it became a refuge for the child who just needed a few moments to escape. Often, my friend would escape her brothers by peeling back the tarp that covered the little rowboat and climbing in to lie at the bottom, daydreaming.

One mother's creativity at "making do" made memories and happiness for her children. When they eventually sold that old boat, then long unused, it was as if they were selling a bulky family heirloom.

We hear it all the time, but it is still true: Children can thrive without stuff, but they cannot survive without love. Love comes through despite financial or other hardships when we use our inventiveness and resourcefulness with our children. Fun is making memories that last a lifetime, enjoying one another's company and working together toward a common goal. It isn't all about fancy trips and who's got the newest video game. It's about how you love your kids, not what you buy them.

Rocks for Sale

Formula for success: Rise early, work hard, strike oil.
—attributed in several sources to J.Paul Getty

*At my lemonade stand, I used to give the first glass away free
and charge five dollars for the second glass. The refill contained
the antidote. —Emo Philips, comedian*

When I was nine years old, Tina lived across the street from us. She lived on a wooded lot, in a yellow house with a brown garage door and brown shutters. We lived in a white two story, and often we'd play in the snow or collect pretty leaves from the piles in our yards.

There were other kids on the block, of course, but I liked Tina best. Her parents always had Fudgesicles in their refrigerator, and they'd let us each eat one, even right before dinner. Tina was a nice kid, about a year younger than I, and she was my best friend.

When the two eleven-year-olds on the block decided to make money starting a lemonade stand, Tina and I put our heads together to come up with our market niche. After a long, long time in kid time, like five minutes, we came up with it! We'd sell rocks!

Now these weren't your ordinary garden-variety junky rocks. Oh, no. We were smarter than that! These were your high quality, glossy rocks. We made the old pebbles we found absolutely shine by rubbing them with soap and dropping them into water. We made them look bright and shiny by displaying them all along Tina's brown garage door in little glass jars of water on TV trays we'd taken from Tina's mother's den.

Tina's father, from whose garden we had taken the majority of the rocks, bought several, and we gleefully counted our pennies. My dad came across and bought two of the big ones. Soon, we'd made 27 cents each! We were living the high life!

Unfortunately, there were no other customers that day, although our mothers were liberated from our presence during store hours. Finally, we closed shop for the day. We congratulated ourselves on being entrepreneurs, even though we didn't know that was the word for our enterprising day.

Those moments selling rocks gave me my first taste of making my own money. I liked it. I liked the feeling that if I did something clever, I could get paid for it. A few years later, it was a paper route, and at fifteen, I started my first "real" business, hiring other kids to do yard work under my supervision, to pay for my college education.

Teaching kids the value of money is harder in our society than it was when we were kids. If you live off checks from your ex, chances are your child is getting a very different view of how money is made than when you were a kid and you saw your dad come home tired from work every night.

There are opportunities everywhere to expose your child to the value of money, better ways perhaps than garnishing savings out of their allowance, although that's one. Earning money from other people is a thrill for kids in their "tweens," especially if an older sibling has already moved on to McDonald's or other "real" work.

Perhaps your child could become involved in Girl Scouts or Boy Scouts, and you can encourage them to sell more candy bars or cookies or car washes than they thought they could. Perhaps they could start a lemonade stand, or run errands for people in the apartment building you live in, or maybe you'd let your kid do what little Matthew did on my block.

Matthew knocked on our door one day and asked if he could take my dog for a walk. My rambunctious year-old dog was always looking for a new person to drag through the neighborhood, so I said a hearty YES! Matthew and Lucky took off down the road.

Matthew is perhaps ten and Lucky has the strength of a wild wolf when he wants to use it. He dragged the poor child up one street and down another, but eventually they returned, each still on his respective end of the leash.

I gave Matthew a dollar, and he told me he was starting a business. Could he come back at the same time tomorrow? By the end of the month, ten-year-old Matthew had four assistant dog-walkers and nearly a dozen dog customers! This kid went from being shy and rather disconnected from life to being engaged and enterprising!

Think back to your first job—remember the thrill of that first paycheck? Perhaps now would be a good time to start letting your child see the joy of work and earning his or her own way in the world, at least a few dollars or so that doesn't come out of your purse. The self-esteem lessons alone might be life changing.

The Surprising Return

One out of four people in this country is mentally imbalanced. Think of your three closest friends. It they seem OK, then you're the one. —Ann Landers, columnist

I'm furious about the Women's Liberationists. They keep getting up on soapboxes and proclaiming that women are brighter than men. That's true, but it should be kept very quiet or it ruins the whole racket. —Anita Loos, writer

I've been rich and I've been poor. Rich is better.
—Sophie Tucker, singer

Sometimes, I think of myself as a stingy person. I try to store up energy and money and other resources for myself. I try to provide enough for my child and me, and to tell the truth, I engage in hoarding behavior. I hoard all sorts of things, hoping that this will prevent me from needing something I don't have in the future. I am well aware this comes out of a real fear of poverty borne out of my childhood.

That self-awareness doesn't seem to stop the behavior.

A few years ago, I experienced a change in my financial circumstances. The change was dramatic enough to make me alter my behavior. I noticed that I suddenly was generous to others. I was tipping generously, not worrying about $5 or $10 here or there, no longer counting every penny.

The results were profound. Suddenly, not only did everything seem much smoother in my life, but little crises were somehow solved immediately. By not clinging to that desperate last $20, I was able to save my child and myself from discomfort and a lot of hassles. When my daughter wanted to jump in the water for a swim but we didn't have a swimsuit in the car, I agreed she could do it fully clothed. We were sixty miles from home! My normal actions afterward would have been to try to wrap her in whatever dry things we may have had in the car, things like my sweater or that spare lightweight blanket we drag everywhere with us. She would have had the fun of swimming, but we would have had to go home immediately thereafter to get her some dry clothes.

This time, we stopped by an inexpensive department store and bought a new package of panties (she needed them anyway, I reasoned), and a sundress. Total expense: $19. In return for $19, which sometimes had been a fortune to us, she got to spend the afternoon swimming *and* enjoy the remainder of the day in new, dry clothing.

It set me thinking on the way home. Sometimes I "strain a gnat to swallow a camel." I think that expression means focusing on the wrong details and making yourself miserable. Sometimes, I focus more on housecleaning than playing dolls. Sometimes, I focus more on making the bed than on making a friend smile. Sometimes, I think more about what I should be doing than what I am doing. Sometimes, I save a few bucks but feel sad, if a few dollars wealthier.

But I notice when I catch myself and choose to change how I've been acting, the world changes with me. I get the book deal I didn't expect. My child picks me a bouquet of wildflowers for no special reason. I find the other one of my long-lost favorite socks hidden folded in a spare blanket. Someone gives my child a gift.

It's curious how this works, and since it is not always cause equals effect at once, it's easy to forget that we all get what we give. When we give love and generosity and peace and happiness, it comes pouring back. When we give fatigue and anger and frustration and miserly spending, we get more of that.

You've probably heard that "what you focus on becomes your reality." When we focus on lack, on not enough, on the bad things, that's what we receive in good measure. But when we focus on the positive, on giving, on smiling whether we feel like it or not, when we hold that purse perhaps a little less tightly, every now and then the sunshine of life can pour through and warm our hearts. Focus on the good things, and you'll see more of them.

Graduation Day

Prejudices, it is well known, are most difficult to eradicate
from the heart whose soil has never been loosened or fertilized
by education; they grow there, firm as weeds among stones.
—*Charlotte Brontë, author*

Home is where one starts from. —*TS Eliot, author*

Carin's face was shining with pride, but there were tears in her eyes while she told me the story of her graduation from single parenting. This late-forties mother of one was telling me the story of her daughter, Elise, graduating from high school. The sun glowed through the window and cast soft shadows on the wood table. Our coffee mugs served as sundials while we talked of motherhood.

"The day she graduated from high school, age seventeen, was the tenderest experience of my life with her," she said. "It was a highly emotional day for me because it was the end of a type of parenting I'd been doing her whole life and the beginning of a new type of parenting."

She smiled at me through eyes now glistening with the memory. "It was incredibly emotional because I was proud and happy that Elise was getting out of high school and that she was going to college, but now she would have to go through early adulthood, with all its pain and joys and learning. It was changing my life and hers, forever. It was The End of one thing and The Beginning of another."

Not understanding, because I am nowhere near that day, I offered that perhaps it would be a new lease on life for her, a chance to start over, remake her career, or take up hobbies or travel or do any of the things parents of elementary-school-aged children fantasize they will do someday.

Carin smiled and took a sip of her cooling coffee. "It's not like that in the beginning," she says. "There's so much you are used to doing for your child, so much to be concerned about. What if she calls and I'm not there and she really needs me? And she doesn't even call! You jump every time the phone rings; you worry every time it doesn't." She laughs at herself. "You get over that part."

"I guess I expected to graduate, too, when she did," she said. "I thought she'd come rushing over to me like they do in the movies, and say, 'Mom, I know we went through some hard times, but thanks. You're the best!' That didn't happen.

"Her gratitude didn't come until much later," Carin said. "I had made a point of kissing her good night every night all the way through high school, so we always had that moment where we'd hug and she'd give me a kiss back," she explained. "It was good for her to see such stable affection and expression of love from me, no matter whether we'd had a fight that day or not. All that 'don't go to bed angry' stuff.

"I didn't know it meant as much to her as it did to me," she said, "but then the summer ended and she was away for good. We both went through a lot of changes within ourselves. In her junior year of college, Elise went to Lille to study French. From there, she wrote me a note telling me how much she appreciated me and all the things I'd done for her, and how she wanted to treat any children she might have as well as I did her! I still have that letter in my drawer. It was a real expression of how thankful she was that I had been there for her her whole life. She said that even though she seemed not to like it plenty of times, it meant a lot to her that I always kissed her good night. It was really touching."

Carin smiled thoughtfully and gazed out the window for a moment, soft memories floating all around her. Her daughter will graduate from college in a few months and is already engaged. Carin has realized she isn't needed in the same way anymore, and she's remade her life. She's more involved with her church and dates a wide variety of men "just for fun," and she even started a new line of products in the company she owns. I admire how she capably did it all by herself from the time her daughter was four until now. I know some of the sacrifices she made, and I've watched her grow and mature.

"Carin, what did you learn from parenting Elise?" I asked my friend. "If you had one thing, just one, what would you tell a mom with younger kids?"

My friend sat back thoughtfully and twiddled her coffee cup in circles for a moment. "I guess I've learned it isn't so much the method of how you parent. What counts is how able you are to express your love for your child. Everyone parents differently. The one consistent thing that makes the bond strong is the parent's ability to let the child know on a daily basis how much they are loved. It has to be a daily thing. Every day, your child has to know that you love him or her, no matter how angry you've gotten at one another. It's harder when they are teens, but that's when it seems to pay off most."

"It isn't about words so much," she says. "It's not sitting there and going 'I love you I love you I love you.' I believe that our job as parents is to always surround our children with loving light, to always make them feel loved and protected, even when they are being difficult or unloving toward us."

I believe, like Carin does, that being consistent in our love for our kids is the most important thing we can do as parents. Always having an open heart and letting your child know just how much he or she means to you gives them a foundation to last a lifetime. Some day we will graduate from Parenting 101: Parenting a Child and move on to Parenting 201: Parenting a Young Adult. The relationship will change, but the foundation of love and communication we are building now will last a lifetime.

Knocking Up Opportunity

And then the day came when the risk to remain tight in a bud
was more painful than the risk it took to blossom.
—Anaïs Nin, *author*

Since I was twenty-four there never was any vagueness in my
plans or ideas as to what god's work was for me.
—Florence Nightingale, *nursing pioneer*

Jackie tells me she'll come when I invite her to a holiday party at my house next Saturday. I assure her there will be some single men there.

"Oh, I don't care about that," she insists immediately. "I don't have time for anyone in my life right now." She goes on to tell me about little league and swimming classes for her fourth-grade son, and how with work hours and trying to juggle everything she doesn't even have time for herself. "I'm so tired at night, I think that having a man in my life would only make things much, much worse," she tells me confidently.

The party comes and so does Jackie. During the evening, she meets my neighbor, Dave, a nice professional man with a big house just down the block. I see them chatting on and off during the evening.

The next morning, Jackie sends me an e-mail. "What do you know about Dave?" she writes. I tell her what little I know, and she writes back again, almost immediately, asking me if I think he is interested in her. I have absolutely no idea, so I tell her "Maybe. I saw him talking to you often. I'll give you his e-mail address if you like."

She writes back again within five minutes and tells me, "Well, I don't like him at all. He didn't even come to the door to say good night to me when I left your party."

Forgive me if I'm mistaken, but is this the same woman who didn't want a relationship and had no time for a relationship, and who now kind of started to like an eligible man and immediately slammed the door on even speaking to him again?

I wonder in which areas of my life do I do one thing and say another? I wonder what doors I slam before they even open. I wonder how many ways I shut myself off to opportunities because I have some preconceived notion about what someone should look or act like, or what a situation should seem to be from the first moments. I wonder how often I wait for "the perfect time" and then feel frustrated because it doesn't come.

My friend Mark Victor Hansen, coauthor of the *Chicken Soup for the Soul* series and author of many other wonderful books and inspiring tape programs, told me a story. After one of his seminars about creating the life you want, a woman came up to him. She complained, "Mr. Hansen, I'd love to go back to college, but it will take five more years to get the degree I want. I'll be forty-three by the time I get out!"

Wisely, Mark Victor told her, "How old will you be in five years if you don't go back to college?" Mark and all the other teachers, coaches and success motivators throughout history have always taught us that NOW is the time to take action, to begin the life you seek.

It's never too late to begin having the life you want. It's

never too late to open yourself to new opportunities. It's never too late to start living. It's never to late to have a happy tomorrow!

When I left my husband, I did it partly because a trusted counselor told me, "Do you want to set an example of a mother who sticks it out even if she's miserable, or of someone who takes control of her life and her own happiness?" I chose the latter. Whether it is about finding a man, going back to school, changing jobs, or some other major life decision, only you can control what happens, only you can seize the opportunities life arrays before you.

Some people say opportunity only knocks once, I think it keeps on knocking and knocking and knocking. It's largely a matter of being ready to open the door, just a crack, and see what's out there. Take a chance on your own happiness. Now is the perfect moment to begin!

Dark Night of the Soul

*Never leap ahead of grace, but wait for grace and quietly
follow with the gentleness of the Spirit of God.*
—Sister Helen Prejean, author, Dead Man Walking

*When we are talking to God, we're praying. When
God is talking to us, we're schizophrenic.*
—Lily Tomlin, comedian, actor

Where is grace when we need it anyway? Where is the hope
of tomorrow when today seems so bleak? Sometimes when
we are facing depression, loss, sadness, or loneliness, the
world seems a dark and frightening place. These are the
times known as the "dark nights of the soul," the times
when we sit in silence and suffer alone in most cases.

In these moments, single mothers can feel their alone-
ness cover them like a blanket of snow. There are moments
when the burdens of life make a person wish for a better
tomorrow. In these times it always helps us to see how we
are progressing overall. One dark moment or two does not
a bad life make.

They say the greatest sense of loneliness is not in being
alone, but in being in a bad relationship and lonely in it.
Perhaps you can relate to that comment? Everyone, married,
single, parent, or not, feels such times of sadness in life.
Usually, there is no person at fault. Nor is the cause outside
ourselves. In fact, attaching a cause to these dark moments
does not illuminate our path, rather it forces us to make
decisions when we are not in a healthy place emotionally.

Such periods of depression always end someday. We go through dark times, and we go through bright times. There are seasons in every life, seasons that make for a brighter future. This too shall pass. Nothing stays the same while we are alive, no one day is precisely like the one before. And there's always the possibility of a brighter tomorrow. Look back at your life and you will see moments in the sun as well as dark moments you would prefer to have avoided. It's what you do about the dark times that determines the brightness of your future.

I have a friend named W. Mitchell. Mitchell lives in a wheelchair. In his compelling book, *It's Not What Happens to You, It's What You Do about It,* he tells the story of his amazing life. Mitchell is an inspiration to us all.

When he was a young man, he drove his motorcycle right under a semi truck, and it ignited his bike's gas tank. When they pulled him out, he was mostly burned and in terrible pain. There was a huge chance he wouldn't live. But he did, although more than 80 percent of his body was burned.

Mitchell faced hundreds of skin grafts to give him back a face. His fingers had burned off, and he had to have skin planted all over his body. I don't know about you, but I think I would have given up. But he didn't. Talk about a dark night of the soul! But Mitchell was learning how to live life fully, no matter what.

Mitchell went on to live well. He started a company that became hugely successful. He married a beauty queen. He ran for mayor of his Colorado hometown. He built a life out of what literally were the ashes of his previous existence. He had reached a positive season. He even learned to fly a plane!

But nobody stays on top or on the bottom forever.

One day, he was flying the plane with a group of friends. Something went horribly wrong, and the plane crashed! Mitchell ordered his passengers to quickly evacuate the plane. They scrambled out, but Mitchell seemed to be pinned under the wreckage. He struggled to free himself, as he tells it, "terrified that the plane would ignite" and that he'd be burned again.

The plane did not ignite. He wasn't even stuck. His lower vertebrae had been crushed and he was now paralyzed from the waist down—for life. They eventually removed his now useless toes and grafted them on where he used to have fingers.

That's a pretty bleak season in a person's life. But Mitchell's life cycled out of there too. He remarried. He became an internationally recognized professional speaker, inspiring thousands of people every year to make it through the bad spots in their lives. He believed that his amazing stories could save other people from their despair.

In the darkest time of my life, someone gave me a tape of one of his riveting speeches, and it helped me through. Now Mitchell is a beloved friend to me, and a true inspiration to all who meet him. He's a dear, kind man. Find and read his book if you can—or listen to one of his speeches. It illustrates the seasons of life so clearly, and reassures us that we can all positively face whatever is confronting us.

In the dark days of your life, the overwhelming and financially burdensome times, it helps to remember that it isn't about what happens to us, it's about what we do with the times we are facing. It's about believing that a better tomorrow will come, because it always does, and then doing your best in the moment to create a happier future.

Cash on the Barrel Head

Veni, vidi, Visa. (We came, we saw, we went shopping.)
—Jan Barrett, singer, comedian

Wealth is what you accumulate, not what you spend—
Thomas J. Stanley and William D. Danko, authors,
The Millionaire Next Door

Like most people, I have a love-hate relationship with money. I love lots of it, I hate its confines. Rather than continue to feel sorry for myself, I went to a financial management seminar and read a couple dozen books on the subject. My favorite is an incredible book called, *The Millionaire Next Door: The Surprising Secrets of America's Wealthy* by Thomas J. Stanley, Ph.D. and William D. Danko, Ph.D.

I picked up a system that actually works for me. It's amazing how easy the system is, how simple it works, if you have the guts to try it.

Apparently, in America, lots of people do what I used to do. That is, we spend money using checks and ATM cards and credit cards, and only rarely do we touch real green money. Oh, sure, we may stock a couple of $20s from the ATM machine, but we rarely carry real cash.

One way to get in touch with your money is to use cash for an entire month. I know it sounds weird, and what if you get robbed, and some bills cannot be paid in cash. Okay. So pay them with a check like always, and how many people do you know who've been robbed? But for everything else you buy, from groceries to gas, from clothes to Chinese food, pay cash for just one month. Keep the receipts, however small, for every purchase. Write on the back what you bought if the receipt doesn't tell you.

It's a weird feeling to start the day with $60, and at the end of the day not know where it went. It's strange to think that every time you hand over a certain amount of that lovely, lovely green stuff, you are exchanging X hours at work for whatever you are getting.

One way to get in touch with your Inner Spender is to figure out precisely how much per hour your actual after-tax take-home pay is. At the end of your cash-only month, haul out your receipts. Under categories like "Food" and "Entertainment," write down how much you spent, of course, but also list specifics, event by event, item by item. Figure out how much of your life you had to trade for each thing you wanted so bad at the moment of purchase.

Money is only a medium of exchange. You exchange your time and services and brainpower with your employer (or, if self-employed, with your customers) in return for money. Then you trade your time, services, and brainpower turned into cash for other things you want. Duh. You learned that in seventh grade. But how often do you really connect to the fact that you are giving away hours of your life for the things you bring into it?

Is that new knickknack really worth a half hour of your life? Is it worth trading an hour of work time for a pizza? Does driving a car that costs just $75 more a month really change your life, or would you rather use the money on something that will bring you happiness and less stress, and drive a different car that works just fine but might not be as flashy?

Would you rather save the money and use it for something that has more value for you? Would you rather save your money so you can spend time, eventually, doing what you choose instead of what you must? How secure would you feel if you had the nest egg the experts recommend—three to six months of your salary stashed away for a rainy day? How would it feel to wake up without debt tomorrow—or in a year or two? What if you were getting closer to having a down payment on a house for you and the kids? Wouldn't that be great? Wouldn't you be a lot less stressed out?

Are you setting the right money example for your children? Are you showing them that the consequence of hard work is enough money to live on, or are you showing them that no matter how hard you work, there will never be enough? Which is more motivating for a young person to observe?

It's your money, it's your life. How will you spend it?

The Road to Truth

Life is too short to wear tight shoes.
—Grandma Ros, folk heroine

*The woman whose behavior indicates that she will make a
scene if she is told the truth asks to be deceived.*
—Elizabeth Jenkins, English writer

"If you look for truth, at no point can you be doing the
wrong thing. If you're searching for truth, even when you
are mistaken you are being guided appropriately," my philo-
sophic friend settles back into the chair. "Truth isn't a
utopian ideal, it is something that has it's own intrinsic
value, outside your own wishes. After you understand that
things are, they just are, things are easier. They just are."

Could life become easier if I live the truth? I'd do a lot of
things to have an easier life. Is the truth available for experimentation? And what is the truth anyway? Would I know
it if I saw it?

On one level, what you will eat today, what you will do
today, is your truth. Truth is a useful thing. It can affect
world relationships and global politics. It can improve the
quality and value of our lives and personal relationships.
Decide not to lie to yourself today. If you like something,
like it. If you don't like something, don't.

My friend Sandra has a pair of camel-and-black pumps
that I compliment her on. "Thanks," she says. "They are a
half size too small, but I got them on sale. They really hurt."
The truth: the shoes hurt her feet. It's a simple matter, but

if she'd told herself the truth in the store, she would have saved her money for shoes that fit, on sale or not.

Truth isn't My Truth, it's general, universal truth. Truth exists independent of me. I may like something more, you may like something else. I like salsa dancing, you may like waltzing. If everyone lived their truth, we'd save a lot of time, wars, divorce, and child-rearing problems.

Truth comes into play in our lives when we look at our child, who begs for just one more bedtime story. You think about how tired you are, and how you were really looking forward to a hot bath. Oh, well. The child needs a story, and one more won't hurt much. Your truth: you'd rather take a hot bath. Your nontruth: Choosing to read one more story. Your result: The child can sense your fatigue and learns that she or he can manipulate you, or feels guilty (depending on the child's personal sensitivity to your feelings) for begging for something just to stay up. You're both tired the next day. Was it worth it to lie?

Truth restores our lives. You have a busy work schedule, but they need a mother volunteer for school next week. You're already behind on your projects. You say "Yes" when you'd love to say "Later." Your result: being stressed out and irritable with other people—your coworkers, your children, others. Not having a moment to recharge. Doing the work at the office and the school begrudgingly or poorly. Spreading your unhappiness around. Was it worth it to lie to yourself and others?

Nontruth is dating a man you really don't like very much because you're lonely. You allow him to think perhaps the relationship is progressing even though it really isn't in your heart. Perhaps you allow him too far into your life, or perhaps you just float through the months without really looking at what is true for you: he's not The One you were hoping for. Will it feel better that you didn't tell the truth when you ditch him months later?

Truth seems to save a lot of time and heartache. People who live their truth, and who were raised by parents who lived their truth, tend to be confident achievers who feel more comfortable being genuinely helpful and loving to others because they are doing it from a willing heart. Truth saves irritability, exhaustion, overwork, and annoyance. It's the difference between waking up ready for the day and waking up dreading what you've gotten yourself into. Which will you choose?

A Blizzard of Bliss

Happiness is good health and a bad memory.
—Edith Wharton, author

Ask yourself if it will bring you happiness or pleasure. Pleasure
is fleeting. —His Holiness The Dalai Lama, as quoted in The
Art of Happiness

Happiness can only be lived in the moment. Happiness is being where you are and being glad you are there. Friedrich Wilhelm Nietzsche said in his *Will to Power* that bliss is basically when, "One wants nothing to be different, not forward, not backward, not in all eternity, Not merely to bear what is necessary, but to love it." That is truth, and it is also bliss. It is being happy in the moment regardless of that moment, because that is the moment you are in.

Let me tell you my friend Alexa's story of bliss. Warning: It doesn't sound very blissful. And that's the point. Alexa tells me, "I had a very bad second marriage. I was faced with a situation that I simply could not endure. One day, my second husband kicked me out, along with my son from my first marriage. We divorced quickly, and I pretty much lost everything. He took all the money and hid it somewhere. My whole professional life was the corporation that he had begun and I had worked for, and he was the corporation.

So I suddenly became homeless and jobless. It was the day of a blizzard, and the snow was three feet deep. I had no money and nowhere really to turn. My parents had never approved of this man anyway, so there was no help anywhere. The fact was we were pretty much left out in the snow. I had found an apartment with my last bit of money, and I was hauling stuff from the house we'd shared to the new apartment. My ex had one of his flunkies come and take my car because it was in the corporation's name. My ex was using a lot of drugs, and he was really not mentally stable."

"My son and I had to carry the rest of our stuff from the house to the apartment through the snow, and it was several blocks. My son was eleven or twelve at the time. He's cussing and raising hell, cursing the man who had abandoned us so wickedly, and me for marrying the jerk. I was angry and afraid, too, but I told him 'Let's look at the bright side. 1. You're getting exercise. 2. We don't have to deal with him anymore, ever. Life is great, and it's getting better every second.' I felt liberated because I didn't have to worry about whether he'd been using when I got home from the office at night. I felt so joyful!

"On the way back to our apartment, we stopped at Burger King. I spent $5 on dinner. I have to tell you, it was a better meal than any I had tasted when I was married to Paul. It was the first meal of freedom, and it doesn't taste any better than that! Two years later, we moved to LA and got a fresh new start.

"Sometimes now I'm in a traffic jam in LA in November. I think, I could be in three feet of snow, scared and alone, hauling stuff from a big house into a tiny apartment. I'll never forget that day! I can choose to be happy in the moment, and how I choose is what makes the moment what it is. All that exists is my experience of it. For me, bliss is deciding that where I am, right now, is right where I want to be."

Instant Parenting:
Just Add Water

Fear is that little darkroom where negatives are developed.
—Michael Pritchard, comedian

My grandmother is over eighty and still doesn't need glasses.
Drinks right out of the bottle. —Henny Youngman, comedian

I bought some of that powdered water the other day, but I
don't know what to add. —Stephen Wright, comedian

"I make a lot of mistakes in my life," Monica tells me. She looks down at her hands and then smiles up at me, a little nervously. "Leo and I got married right out of high school, which was the first big mistake. But I was already pregnant, and I really believed we could make it work. We lived in a little tow-behind travel trailer that belonged to my grandma. We parked it on a piece of land Leo's uncle owned way out in the sticks. When I got too pregnant to work, I stayed home and waited to have the baby. I tended our garden of marijuana plants and dreamed that Leo was going to grow up just as soon as the baby was born.

"We had a little boy, and he was the apple of my eye, of course," Monica tells me, her eyes shining at the memory. "But Leo just sort of went nuts. Here was this little baby crying all the time, and we were stuck in this dumb trailer, and he was working to support us by pumping gas. It was a real bad life. We argued nearly all the time and got stoned the rest of it."

Monica tells me how she and Leo were fighting so much he would leave for a week at a time. She started drinking and things got worse. She knew he was having sex with one of her old high school classmates, but she wanted to stay with him because she was pregnant again.

"We got along just enough for me to get pregnant again," she says. "I wasn't ready for motherhood.

"One day a couple months after our second baby was born, Leo's real mom flew in from Connecticut. His dad and stepmom had raised him to be a white trash pig, she announced. He hadn't seen his ma for a couple of years, but she had some kind of hold on him. She told him to leave the kids and me and come back with her, and she'd pay for him to go to college. She had money, too.

"Much to my surprise, Leo said he wouldn't leave the kids," Monica said. "I didn't think he even cared about them, because he left them with me for days at a time. I guess he had more fatherly feelings than I thought.

"His mother went crazy and started screaming. I remember I just sat there, because I was stoned and I'd been drinking. The baby was crying, she was screaming, and Leo was yelling at her. I didn't care. I think that was the worst day of my life.

"Somehow, in the middle of it all, Leo's mom made me a deal. If I'd leave her son alone and let her take Leo and both my sons back to Connecticut to be 'raised properly' she'd give me $2,500 cash and $500 a month for a year.

"I was not even twenty years old. I took the deal, and she took Leo and the kids. We got a divorce really fast, and his mom took care of everything. I stayed in the trailer until

Leo's uncle told me to get off his land. I went through a lot of hell before I saw my boys again, but I thought about them a lot," Monica said. She kept drinking, she continued with drugs, and she took up with lots of wrong men. Finally, around age thirty, she started to straighten her life out with the help of a friend who got her into Alcoholics Anonymous.

"I got my life back together, bit by bit. I went to night school, and I got a good job. I wanted to make amends, so I tracked down my sons in Connecticut. Leo answered the phone."

"When I talked to Leo, I could hear a baby crying in the background. It turns out he'd recently gotten married again, and it was their baby. His mom had died the year before, and the boys, my boys, who she had raised, had become a lot of trouble. We talked for a while, and Leo asked me where I lived. I told him, and I gave him my address and I took his. I wanted to write to my boys, and he said I could call."

"I called them three or four times," Monica said. The boys were eleven and twelve now, and didn't really know who their mother was. She began saving up money to fly to see them or to fly them to see her. They kept in touch for about four months.

"Then one day, I got a call from Leo. He said he'd just gotten back from the airport. My two sons were on their way to my house! He told me he couldn't take care of them anymore, and neither could his new wife. The boys had been in some trouble with the law."

Monica shakes her head. "I didn't even really know what they looked like! They'd sent me recent school pictures, or I wouldn't have recognized my own sons. They both got off the plane, and my heart leapt! These were my boys! They were trying to act tough, like they weren't going through hell and falling apart, but inside they must have been really hurting. I wanted to kiss and cuddle my babies, but these were big boys, nearly young men, so I didn't really know what to do. Leo had made it clear he wasn't planning on taking them back. I didn't know if they knew that or not.

"So here they are, living across the country in California in a whole new life with a woman they've just met, who is their mother. I didn't really have any extra money to support two big boys, and boy, can they ever eat! We did a lot, I mean a lot, of macaroni and cheese suppers.

"I felt sorry for them, uprooted from their whole life. They took turns sleeping on the couch or the floor because I only had a studio apartment when they got here. Suddenly, everything was hard and took so much energy. I had no more social life. I didn't want to leave them home alone because they were unruly, and I was a little afraid of what they might do. Within six weeks, they were already getting into pretty serious trouble. If they'd been in grade school, it would have been easier for them and for me.

"Luckily, I had a friend from AA who offered to help us out with counseling. It took more patience and maturity than I ever thought I had, but I learned to compliment them when they did something well. They started to blossom like flowers that haven't been watered. They eventually started to tell me what their life had been like and to ask tough questions about the choices I'd made in mine."

It hasn't been easy, as you can imagine, but Monica's oldest son will graduate from high school this year. Her love and her willingness to grow personally has changed him dramatically from the boy who first came here, angry and rejected by everyone, into a normal kid. His brother has a milder personality, and he's become an athlete at school, and is making a B average. Overall, she's done very well with the boys. I ask her if she ever wanted to give up.

"Not after Leo sent them back to me. Sure, it was hard—it's the hardest thing I've ever done. But to see your own child smiling and happy, to get a precious hug, that means the world to me. That's the greatest high of all."

Squid Factor

The attractiveness of one is directly proportionate to the ugliness of the other. —Todd Cumberland, amateur philosopher

Among all the absurd forms of courage, the courage of girls is outstanding. Otherwise, there would be fewer marriages. —Colette, French writer

"Have you ever noticed the squid factor in relationships?" Todd asks the random group as he holds court from his seat in the coffee shop. We're his friends, although none of us know one another's last names. We sit scattered randomly across bistro tables and the rattan sofa, perch on bar stools, or stand waiting for mocha lattes.

The place is slow tonight; it's mostly the regulars, and my child is at art class. I have one hour and forty minutes to relax and be one of the gang. I'm first to respond to Todd's question with the obvious, "What's the squid factor?"

Todd tells me it's the difference between people in relationships. It's his own theory and it seems to go something like this: The most handsome, eligible, wealthy, or in other ways desirable men seem to date and marry the most shrew-like, annoying, whining, demanding women.

We all chuckle, thinking about couples we know where this is true. Todd says, "And the most beautiful, desirable, intelligent, poised women seem to marry or date the weirdest guys. They go after the freaks, the ex-cons, the losers and abusers, the substance addicts."

Thinking back to my girlfriends' last beaux and my ex-husband, perhaps he's right. Todd shakes his head. "Whenever you get in a new relationship, or even think about one, you have to ask yourself, 'Is this person a squid'?"

Now, why he uses the term "squid" makes no sense to me whatsoever, but I go back to chatting with my table mate and store Todd's comments for when I see myself about to sink into the infatuated stage in a relationship.

Soon enough, I haul out his curious moniker and ask myself, "Is this guy a squid?" Of course, it would be great if I had a Squid Detector and could detect the guys from a mile away who fit this strange label. I'd save myself a lot of trouble. In fact, my whole life would have gone differently.

My child has a built-in squid detector, I noticed. I introduce her to a new guy and she says, "Mom, he's so not your type." I am getting relationship advice from a kid! During a difficult breakup, we were singing along to a song in the car. The woman insists she needs a lover who won't drive her nuts, a guy who isn't going to hurt her. My daughter says, "Mom, Mom! Listen to what she's saying! This is your song, Mom. Listen to her." I ditch the guy. He was on his way out, anyway.

Where did my Squid Detector get buried? Did I suddenly become unable to tell a great guy from a bad one on my thirtieth birthday? Is your Squid Detector intact, or do you pick guys who turn out to be creeps, users, and losers?

I found my Squid Detector tossed in the bottom of a rusty old trunk buried at the bottom of my heart. Inside the box were things like Lost Loves, Memories of Men Who Left Me, vestiges and wisps of memories of Men I Dumped, pictures of "ideal men" like Brad Pitt and Pierce Brosnan, the list of four hundred characteristics the Ideal Man must possess for me to be truly interested, and other romantic artifacts from my life.

It began working fine once I washed it down with some strong cleanser and squirted some W-D 40 into the movable parts. I keep it in my gut. They say you know what a guy's problems are and whether he's worth it in the first ten minutes of meeting him if you're listening. The listening is where the Squid Detector comes in.

If you listen to what he says, the Squid Detector will start humming, buzzing, whirring, and flashing red warning signals if he's a bad guy. If he's a good guy, you get the yellow caution light, which means "Go slowly, girlfriend!"

See if you can determine which of these lines, casually tossed out in the first ten minutes of conversation by real men, indicate a high level of Squidness.

"My ex-wife, that stupid bitch! She took everything I had, and she still wants more!" (He'll be saying bad things about you in a few years.)

"You are the most beautiful woman I've ever seen! I'm falling in love with you already!" (Isn't this is a little sudden, no matter how flattering it is?)

"I've got two kids, but I never see them. I'm really busy at work, and it's just so hard to get away." (How in the world will he have time for a life with you if he treats his own children with such disdain?)

"I'm not really quite all the way divorced yet, but we're in negotiations." (Give him your number if you must, and tell him to call you in two years.)

"I pay X in alimony. It's killing me!" (Talking about his financial woes in the first few minutes is a big, big warning sign.)

"I've been single my whole life," the forty-seven-year-old man says. "I guess I just haven't been lucky enough to find the right woman yet." (Does the term "commitment-phobic" mean anything to you?)

Did you guess D), all of the above are Squids? Good for you! Your Squid Detector is working just fine. Single Moms haven't got a moment to waste on the wrong guy. Whether or not you want to remarry or have more children, you cannot afford the emotional and psychic drain of dating the wrong guys while you are trying to single-handedly parent your children!

Next time you are chatting with an interesting new guy, ask yourself whether he's a Squid, and then listen for your Squid Detector to sound off the answer. It'll save you and your children a lot of time and unhappiness.

One Who Kisses

Why won't you let me kiss you good night? Is it something I said?—Tom Ryan, comedian

I wasn't kissing her, I was whispering in her mouth.
—Chico Marx, comedian

In French, there is an adage that roughly translates to, "There's always one who kisses, and one who offers the cheek," which I interpret as meaning there's always one person way more interested in the relationship than the other.

The interesting thing is, this applies not only to relationships with a man, but also to relationships with other women. Many of us have "hangers-on," also called "energy suckers," people who will use our time, money, babysitting help, resources, or energy, but who don't really provide any value to us in return. These are people who invade our boundaries and take a big piece of our emotional energy, even though we don't want them to. I have a friend who I yank myself away from regularly. We start casually chatting again. Then she gets into a crisis, and wham! Suddenly she's calling three times a day for half an hour each time—while I'm working. Then I scrape her off again. Do you know anyone like this?

Maybe it's our mother, who allegedly is just "checking in" or "helping out" but who demands vast amounts of emotional or psychic energy in return. Perhaps it's a coworker whose troubles never seem to end, who drains you every time you speak with her about her life. Maybe it's a man you're dating who you constantly have to prop up, reparent, and help out emotionally. Are you holding his hand through a messy divorce? Has he just not yet quite grown up? Do things need to be on his terms and at the times he's available?

Psychologists refer to "boundaries" in our lives as being how far we can be pushed or coerced into doing something against our will, and knowing ourselves well enough to know our own desires. Apparently, the ideal is to create firm boundaries so you can't be borrowed for someone else's agenda, used up, and then left empty.

As single moms, I think we are especially vulnerable to manipulation. Most of us sacrifice a great deal for our child on a daily basis. Think about it: If your child needs help with homework but you really wanted to crash in front of the TV after an awful day at work, which will you do? Most moms will do the homework, and I'm not suggesting we shouldn't.

But there are a lot of grownups out there to whom you actually owe nothing. We cannot apply the same energetic allowances to other adults that we do to our children. There are a lot of people who, consciously or subconsciously, with malice of forethought or completely obliviously, would love to use your energy and resources and give you next to nothing in return.

The culprit may be the nice neighbor lady who loves to talk to you about how the repairman made a mistake fixing her plumbing. Or it could be a girlfriend who has a string of problems she never actually solves and always begs you to listen to.

You know who they are. The energy suckers are the people who come into your life, latch onto your good heart, and use you up for their own purposes. "There's always one who kisses, and one who offers the cheek" applies to you if you are the one who dreads it when the phone rings at 8 P.M. nearly every night, just at bedtime story time, and it's your mother or your friend and you neglect yourself, your responsibilities, or your child to meet another person's needs.

You have plenty of responsibilities: your child(ren), yourself, your bills, and other legitimate obligations. Practice saying "No" kindly to the people who are using you. This will help you erect boundaries by fencing off your life from misuse by people who give you nothing in return. Think of your life as a hot air balloon. How high can you fly when you're loaded down with cargo you don't need?

Allow yourself to stake out your own territory. If your major interruptions and disruptions come from your child, it's okay to say, "I'm going to take a hot bubble bath for fifteen minutes. Please leave me alone unless you or your sister get hurt." It's fine to tell your mother, "Mom, I'm reading to Samantha and Jack now, and then I'm going to bed early. Let's talk on the weekend." It's even correct to say to a friend, "Marisa, I'd love to talk, but right now I need a little time to reenergize. I had a really long day at work. Let's get together over coffee break tomorrow, okay?" You can even tell your PTA, "No, I'm sorry. I cannot help set up for the Valentine's Day party this year. I'm just overwhelmed at work right now. But call me for the Halloween party." If you don't, and your life is still out of control, you have no one to blame but the worn-out woman in the mirror.

It's okay to stake out time for yourself, time to give your child, and time for you and your child to be together. It will give you strength and power you can only imagine now. Take a moment to think of the people you dread talking to and the obligations you're in that you'd rather not have. These are the areas where you are merely offering the cheek. Even list them on a sheet of paper, and estimate how much time you spend with them in a given month. Ask what you are getting from them. If it just isn't worth it, take responsibility for yourself! Reclaim that time using the very powerful little word "No." You might find a whole new world of respect and effectiveness and energy awaits you.

Parallel Lives

In my long and colorful career, one thing stands out: I've been misunderstood. —Mae West, early feminist icon

Capital punishment is either an affront to humanity or a potential parking place. —Larry Brown, novelist

Today Margie called and told me about her friend who is raising her husband's seventeen-year-old son with him. When she married him, she brought into the marriage three smaller children of her own. His son just tried to commit suicide today, just tried to end a life that pains him horribly. His mother died when he was young, and now that his father is remarried to a woman much stricter and more religious than his mother, this young man is in pain. He's crying out for help—he's screaming out for help—and no one can help him.

Margie tells me that they impose such a strict curfew on the boy that when he is one minute late, they lock him out of the house for the night. The stress on the kid must be intense. Then there's his repeated stealing and attempts to kill himself and his sense of loneliness and rebellion. The boy's in pain, and although people see it, no one can reach in and solve his problems. It's easy to wonder why they don't seek professional help. They apparently are out of their depth with the child. What kind of adult will he become if he makes it that far? A recluse? A delinquent? A criminal? So depressed he has to spend his life in treatment?

Years ago, a middle-aged man with thinning brown hair and a fearful expression on his face lived on my block. He lived in a white house with peeling paint and an overgrown evergreen hedge so high that you couldn't see the house from the sidewalk. He rarely came out in the daylight. He hid in there with aluminum foil over all the windows—it must have been pitch black inside! He hoarded newspaper, according to one neighbor. According to another, he'd lived with his mother and inherited the house when she died. He'd supposedly kept her body a week before he turned it in to the morgue.

I saw the man once or twice in the six years I was his neighbor. He was as pale as a bug that lives deep in the dirt. He had wild hair and huge, abnormally round eyes. The little kids on the block were afraid of him, afraid to pass his house, and I could see why.

I don't know how he got food, unless he walked the blocks to the bus stop. The greasy driveway with long, tall wavy blades of grass growing between the cracks had one very old car with a flat tire that never moved an inch. The neighbor who owned the house right beside his tried to get the fire marshal to condemn the place, because he said it was stacked floor to ceiling with debris and old newspaper. The strange guy never waved back the few times I saw him. I still wonder what was wrong with him, what made him seem so afraid, and how his parents raised him to create such a maladjusted man—or was it something physically wrong?

This month there was a story in our newspaper of a woman who parked her ancient, dilapidated RV on the beach. A neighbor saw a number of cats crawling about the place, and being an animal advocate, he called the humane society. They found thirty-four cats living inside the small travel trailer! The paper reported cat feces was more than six inches deep on the floor, the stench was intolerable, and there was not enough drinking water set out for all the animals. In their removal, they found three dead cats stuffed in various places in the RV. The woman was taken for observation. Her family refused to comment.

How did these three people get off the track? Will the seventeen-year-old in the first story become the strange man in the second? Will the strange man in the second continue like the cat lady in the third? How many people in our communities live on the fringe?

Whether by mental imbalance, chemical imbalance, or some other reason, it seems to me a lot of people are forced to live on the fringe. Their own pain engulfs them and makes them feel alone, lonely, vulnerable, and afraid. They become "weird" and are shunned by society.

Sometimes, as a single mom, I feel alone too. My single-with-no-kids friends seem to have endless hours to get their hair done and go to parties and sleep in. My married friends always have something going on. I sometimes feel like an outcast, like I don't really fit into any social group and don't really have time to go anywhere anyway.

When pondering this social problem one day, it occurred to me that I know a lot of people who feel the same way. There's the guy who's been single for seven years since the love of his life dumped him. There's the quirky business-man who thinks he's Don Juan (but isn't). There's the unsmiling woman who moved here from out of state two years ago and still doesn't know a soul. When I looked around, I realized there were plenty of people on the fringe along with me.

So you know what I did? I had a party. Yep, that's right. And now I've done it lots of times, because it works so well. My house isn't fancy, and it isn't all fixed up the way Martha Stewart would do it if she owned it. I don't have a whole lot of extra cash. But once or twice a year, I throw a party and I invite everybody. I invite the angry teenagers and their beleaguered parents, I invite the semi-strange person who lives on my new block, I invite "normal" couples and "typical" single people, and I invite single moms and single dads and their kids and everybody.

It's always fascinating to me to see who shows up. I ask people to bring a drink or a food item, and I make some things, too, and open bags of chips. It's a lot of fun and people feel included and, somehow, the mix of twenty or thirty people or so in my living room kind of gives people a chance to not be the "weird one" or the "boisterous one." They all sort of blend together and bounce into one another and then they leave.

And I clean up the mess. And the phone rings. And it's one after the other calling to tell me what fun they had, and to thank me, and sometimes to invite my child and me to their house or out somewhere else. I created my own community. It reminds me of the saying, "If the mountain won't come to Mohammed, Mohammed will go the mountain."

By folding people into our lives, even if they have "rough

edges," and by making ourselves "part of the gang," we create friendship bridges and opportunities we never had before. The Bible says, "To have friends, you must show yourself friendly." (Proverbs 18:24) People become ostracized from society because they are too chicken to show themselves friendly. The teenage boy isn't mature enough to recognize the distance he's putting between himself and the only people who care about him. The newspaper neighbor and the cat lady had a chance to be normal once, but somehow forgot the basic truth: that our lives are about giving, not hoarding. Life is about opening our hearts and lives to others and living in an authentic way, as nonjudgmentally as we can.

Why not throw a party at your place? Your kid will probably surprise you by helping out for the sake of candy, ice cream, or other treats sure to be there. Or a teen may do it just because it's so freaky that Mom is taking the initiative to get a life.

Invite your friends, your neighbors, your landlord, and the nice checker at the grocery store, more people than you think you know. Invite a wide group of people, from all walks of life, and see if spreading some sunshine and making everyone feel included doesn't immediately take away your sense of being separate, the feeling of you and your kid against the world. It's amazing how warmly people respond to an invitation of friendship. The world is full of good people all around you who are just hoping someone else will take the first step to friendship and warmth. Who knows what good things will transpire from your choice?

I'll Leave the Light On for Ya

*Giving parties is a trivial avocation, but it pays
my dues for my union card in humanity.*
—Elsa Maxwell, writer, famed hostess

Start every day off with a smile and get it over with.
—W.C. Fields, comedian

Not too many years ago, there was a commercial for a discount hotel chain. They hired an actor with a warm and welcoming voice to talk about the simple pleasures of staying in one of the chain's inexpensive rooms. His plain country accent almost lulls the listener into imagining he's right there talking to you and that he's completely sincere in what he's saying.

Especially when he gets to the end.

Like a real country welcome, and to underline the sincerity of his offer, he says in closing, "We'll leave the light on for ya." Now, we both know he was paid to read what some clever marketing scriptwriter came up with. But think for a moment about the ingenuity of that line. It reminds the listener of a truly welcoming place they visited, or of a rural farm in the middle of a picturesque scene. I imagine a comfortable, homespun room, with a handmade heirloom quilt neatly spread across an old bed and common, decent, kind people waiting for me to show up. These folks are early risers and hard workers, but to accommodate your stay at whatever time you might arrive, and to act as a welcome beacon to their visitor in the weary, lonely dark night, they'll "leave a light on for ya."

I wonder whether we as humans can provide that same welcome to other people. I wonder whether we have left the light on in our hearts for others to come in and love us, or whether we've turned it off and sit in blackness, alone, miserable, and defiant.

Today I stood outside of Toys "R" Us waiting for them to open. I wanted to buy my child a much-desired Christmas present, and they'd just put it on sale. I waited with two other women. One was probably in her mid-thirties, with soft, smooth-looking skin, warm brown eyes and neatly dressed-up hair. She was holding a squirmy two-year-old who wanted to get down right there, not realizing it was near a crowded intersection. She looked friendly, the kind of woman you could stop and chat with and find her pleasant. She'd left the light on; it was apparent.

Beside her stood another woman, as if to mark the contrast between light and dark. She looked haggard and angry and a bit scared. They were probably about the same age, but this one looked older. She seemed unhappy, worn out, like she'd been doing dishes all day for the last fifteen hours. I felt sorry for her, and repelled by her at the same time. She obviously had *not* left the light on. She was pushing an infant in a stroller, a happy little girl about ten months old. I wondered how the child would grow up— would she imitate her mother or the friendly woman?

The friendly woman walked right up to the dour one and started a conversation about children. She was so busy being friendly she didn't seem to notice it took the other woman a few minutes to warm up to her. In a few moments, both were chatting. I saw the dull-faced woman smile.

Are you the kind of person who approaches strangers, or are you the one who waits to be approached? If you are neither, and you're more introverted, do you at least walk around with a pleasant look on your face and a smile to share? Do you have a light on so women, and men, can come up and talk to you? It's easier to make friends when you leave a light on for them.

Whether it's meeting a new Mr. Right or just making your life more pleasant to live, whether it's finding a new girlfriend to hang out with or getting better service at the store, try smiling and being extra pleasant. Let your eyes be bright, and think to yourself, "I'll leave a light on for ya!" for the people you will meet today.

Time to Fly

If you look good and dress well, you don't need a purpose in life. —Robert Pante, fashion consultant

Last night I dreamed I ate a ten-pound marshmallow, and when I woke up, my pillow was gone.
—Tommy Cooper, comedian

We boarded a plane today, just moments after the sun peaked over the horizon. My daughter and I struggled through the narrow aisles with our burden of luggage. We bumped past the usual variety of other travelers, all tired from the early morning trip to the airport.

We found our seats and settled in. I was half hoping she'd be tired enough to doze on the plane, but that was not to be. Her little nose pressed against the glass, she oohed and aahed at the ships in the harbor as we circled from LAX out over the Pacific. She marveled at the vistas of clouds and the tiny houses. She told me about cumulus clouds and clouds that carry rain and the third grade version of the hydrological cycle. I smiled, drowsy but pleased.

This isn't the first time she's flown. She's done this many times, in fact. But I travel a lot for business, so to me it is just one long hassle of bumping people and being bumped. To her it was An Adventure.

Sometimes I get so destination-driven, on the ground and in the air, that I forget to take a moment to see the journey of life through the eyes of my child. I forget to get excited about the color of the clouds and their shape. I forgot to press my nose against the window in the thrill of just being.

As if to underline the subtle lesson she is teaching me, she tells me she's hungry and warns me that seven peanuts do not fill her up. (How does she know there will only be seven?) I promise breakfast when we land in forty-five minutes. She immediately complains. "I don't want breakfast; I want to swim at the hotel!" I agree she can do both. "But I want to swim first!"

I laugh. "Aren't you hungry? It's 9 A.M. and you haven't had any breakfast."

She looks at me seriously, as if she doubts my mental stability. "Mom," she says sternly, "swimming is *way* more important than eating!"

Jenny Craig couldn't have said it better herself!

A few minutes later, she knocks me out of my concentration on this vignette.

"Look at the sky, Mom!"

"We're inside a cloud, honey." I reassure her complacently.

"Yeah, but look up! There's the sky!"

Sure enough, a patch of bright blue shows up right above our window.

"If we went up just a little more, we'd crash into the sky! Then it would break into pieces, and they would fall to the ground." She smiles a broad grin, knowing she's being cute.

I marvel at how I got so busy I forgot Chicken Little. I wonder how I forgot to look at the depth of the blue and wonder where the sky begins and ends. I admit, I sometimes also forget to think about ants, and whether or not a horse would fit in my bedroom, and how many birds it would take to lift me off the ground on a ride.

Maybe the things I think are so important are not so important after all. Maybe whether the numbers in my checkbook balance and whether or not there is dog hair on my suit and whether I finished the dishes and whether we should get a new washing machine this year are not the most important things.

What would it be like to take a day, an hour, or even a moment to wonder about what would happen if a plane hit the blue part of the sky?

The Wedding Dress

A lady's imagination is very rapid. It jumps from admiration to love, from love to matrimony in a moment.
—Jane Austen, novelist

I've married a few people I shouldn't have, but haven't we all?—Mamie van Doren, actor

Sometimes, I imagine my eight-year-old is really my confidante, the way an adult would be. Perhaps this comes from having only her consistently in my life since we left her dad six years ago.

This became most apparent to me over the matter of the wedding dress. I was dating someone new, someone more significant than any man who had preceded him. As I grew to like this man more, and he became familiar with my house, my dog, and most of all, my child, I began to think that perhaps, at last, this was a man with whom I could have a lasting relationship and with whom I would not want to tear my hair out in frustration every day.

It was on my mind a large part of the time, this almost-shock at finally finding a man I liked well enough to want to keep in my life. One day, my daughter and I were walking in our yard, and I asked what she'd think if I married him someday.

In my head, I'm considering the vast implications on our free time, our time together, the sacrifices and joys of married life, the ways he is helpful, the ways marriage detracts and adds to one's quality of life, and so on. She's thinking about something else. I don't ask what. I don't even really consider what it might be.

"Mom, I think you should definitely marry him. He's nice to us, he treats us with respect, and he loves us."

These last three criteria are the things I've been drilling into her head every single time she watches a Disney fantasy where princes climb through walls or hack through rose thorns to rescue their beloved. These criteria are there, I hope, to prevent her from assuming someday that just because a man is heroic, sexy, daring, or wealthy (or owns a white horse!), he's The One.

Now these three criteria are a logical answer to my question, and I ponder her comments sequentially. Yes, she's right, he is always nice to us. Yes, he treats us both with respect most of the time. And he seems to love us both, which is good, since we're a package deal.

I tell her he would become her stepdad, which she already knows does not interfere with her relationship with her real dad because she has had a stepmom for many years.

She looks at me wisely, and says, "Do you think you'll have a long train?"

A train? What train? My mind jumps into another category.

Now impatient, she asks, "Mom, will your wedding dress have a long train? That's the skirt part of the wedding dress that you pull behind you when you walk."

I catch my own foolishness in asking a child adult things. I tell her no, I'd wear a simple dress and we discuss a matter of much greater importance to her: what the flower girl will wear. She immediately describes the dress she would prefer and how she wants her hair and what color rose petals she would like to scatter.

Foolish me! Here I was thinking of his suitability to be in our life when she's been planning the wedding.

From the depths of maternal wisdom, I tell her "The wedding is just one day, honey. Then you have to live together for the rest of your lives."

She looks at me as if I've completely missed the point of marrying someone after all. I smile at her innocence, and we move on to other, equally important subjects, like whether or not we ever will build a tire swing in the giant tree in our front yard, and why we don't have many ladybugs this year.

Love may be a many-splendored thing, but so are butter-fly wings and how much an ant can carry on its back and whether or not you like the clothes you are wearing today. Part of the joy of childhood that can be put back into grownup life with a simple focus adjustment is to delight in the colorful details of humdrum daily life. Our children can be our docents in the Museum of Wonder if we allow them to be. Eagerly, they will infuse us with their enthusiasm for life and that joy, tempered with our adult minds, might just be the answer to the age-old conundrum, "If I had it to do over again". . .

Crying in the Dark

*I was in a beauty contest once. I not only came in last, I got
hit in the mouth by Miss Congeniality.*
—Phyllis Diller, comedian

Life is just a bowl of pits. —Rodney Dangerfield, comedian

I fell into bed exhausted, an hour late. I didn't like today,
not one little bit. I was tired, angry, cranky, weary of all the
tasks related to my life. I was the PMS poster child. Where
was time for me? When do I get a break? When is it my turn
to sit on the couch and watch a movie for two hours, and
have someone bring me my favorite dinner on a tray? I'd
even like to have to go to bed early—that would be fine.

I laid there in the dark, waves of frustration and guilt
washing over me. How can I be a good mother and want
space for myself at the same time? Why wasn't I more
giving with my child? I've met mothers who can sit down
and play Barbies for three hours straight. I'm not one of
those. Does that mean I'm ruining my child, and she'll be
in therapy in another decade because of my neglect?

Depression is a factor of not getting enough rest, according to some studies. Could it be that enough sleep is possible, and even mandatory, for mothers?

Somehow, at night, our worries and fears about the
present, past, and future can collide and overwhelm us. We
might try to stifle them by watching the news or reading a
book until our eyes slam shut, but most single moms can
relate to the worry and fear part of motherhood without a
lot of imagination required.

Perhaps you've also noticed that at night, things seem worse than they are in the morning. I've made a game for myself. When I am lying in the dark worrying about something, I tell myself I'll set aside thirty minutes tomorrow to concentrate on finding a solution, but that now I want to sleep. I schedule a bit of time during my lunchtime or first thing in the morning to "worry," which to me means describing the problem clearly, on paper, and listing possible solutions to it.

Sometimes my brain obediently rolls over and falls asleep. Other times, I have to go to Step Two. I have to do a trick I learned somewhere called The Worst Things That Could Happen.

I turn my bedroom light back on, grab my journal, and write down as cogently as I can in my exhaustion precisely *what* the problem is in a few words. Then I write down what I'm afraid could happen. Am I parenting properly? Should I be more religious? Will I get evicted from my apartment? Will they foreclose on my house? Will her father get full custody? Will one of us die early? What if that little leak in the downstairs bath is a major problem?

Whatever dire consequences I'm imagining, I write those down. Getting it on paper makes it easier to think about it objectively. Often, this is where I take a short break to cry about it. Not that it helps, but the stress of actually writing down the big, black, scary thing I'm afraid of is enormously releasing.

Then I determine right there, on the spot, that I could survive the worst thing that could happen. I know, like you do, that people are a lot more resilient than we give ourselves credit for. You will survive it, and so will your child.

Let's say you get evicted. First off, it's better than being executed at dawn for a crime you didn't commit and having your child raised by the state to hate your memory. There are plenty of examples in history of this happening, the most famous two I know of being Marie Antoinette, the Queen in France right before the Revolution, and Mary, Queen of Scots.

Marie Antoinette was imprisoned, humiliated publicly, tried for a number of crimes she did not commit, left to starve and freeze in a rat-infested prison (despite the fact that she was hemorrhaging internally), and then her young son the prince was taken by the rebels and paraded before her prison window shouting hate slogans against his parents while dressed in rebel garb. Shortly afterward, she was beheaded. OK, my life isn't that bad.

Mary, Queen of Scots, was an ardent Catholic and an ineffectual ruler in a time when Scotland needed a strong and Protestant queen. Her son grew up thinking his mother was a religious heretic after his aunt, Elizabeth I of England, had his mom beheaded. He, too, was raised to hate his mother.

My life isn't that bad. How about yours?

So if it isn't a matter of being beheaded tomorrow and our child(ren) raised by criminals and murderers, chances are we can survive, right? If you are about to be evicted, God forbid, if you are brave and humble enough to ask for it, there is help all around you. Friends and family may offer you money or a place to stay for a while. The local community might be able to help you out if you appeal to the right people. The yellow pages have shelter information. There is support, there are ways to keep a roof over your heads and at least some food on your table and to get your kid to school each day so you can get a job or the skills to get a job.

If you're facing less of a crisis than those above, surely you can handle it. After all, as long as you're alive you have a chance to make your life better, don't you? You're not a stupid woman or you couldn't have made it this far.

One of my heroes is the motivational speaker Anthony Robbins. He has a great quote: "The past does not equal the future." He preaches this in his Personal Power tape series and has it printed on coffee mugs, tote bags, T-shirts, and hats. It's one of his primary mottoes. He encourages us to believe that just because right now is rough, just because a month ago was even rougher to survive, making a choice and taking actions can create a better tomorrow.

There are plenty of compelling stories about women who overcame everything and climbed the mountain in front of them. Next time you're crying in the dark, feeling like the world is out to get you, try one of the experiments above and see if it doesn't make you feel that much better. And next time you're at the library, pick up a biography of one of the great women of history: Marie Antoinette, Margaret Thatcher, Elizabeth I, Mary Wollstonecraft, Joan of Arc, Theresa of Avila, or any other woman who intrigues you.

Allow those stories of courage, despair, bitterness, and triumph to comfort you that you are not alone and you are not the first woman to endure hardship, nor will you be the first one to find the path out and back into the sunshine of a new day.

The Hamster of Happiness

Some mornings, it just doesn't seem worth it to gnaw through the leather straps. —Emo Philips, comedian

I turned down a date once because I was looking for someone a little closer to the top of the food chain. —Judy Tenuta, author

Sometimes it seems like life is about work. As working mothers, our schedules are very similar to the day before, at least five days a week. Wake up, dress yourself. Get up the kid(s). Dress them, make breakfast, drive to school, and go to work. Work all day. Pick up the kids. Drive to after-school activities. Run some errands. Come home, make dinner, and help with homework. Do the dishes. Tidy up. Supervise teeth brushing. Read a bedtime story, put them to bed, do a few things, get your pajamas on, go to bed so you can do it all over again tomorrow.

Wow, and we thought hamsters had it rough, running around that squeaky, little wheel and never getting anywhere!

A man I was dating said, "I never knew dating a single mom was so relaxing." I couldn't believe he found it relaxing. He said, "Oh, yes. I never have to worry about you being with another man—you don't have time, and I know your schedule, so I know where you'll be every moment of the day."

Oh, yippee. But he is right. Sometimes, the routinized life can feel horribly confining, even boring. And it isn't just us single moms. It's single dads, too, and married couples. Somehow, as grownups, we forget to be spontaneous; we lose the ability to make life fun and allow a life of drudgery to creep up on us until we can no longer recognize alternatives that might be fun. We feel disengaged from ourselves and our wishes and desires and fantasies. We feel like we're the proverbial hamsters on the wheel. Or maybe jealous of the hamster. (Hey, at least he gets to sleep as long as he wants all day in that warm nest in the fragrant wood chips.) How do we find happiness and break out of the rut, get off the wheel, open our lives and hearts to new patterns?

There's an awesome book called *Finding Flow: The Psychology of Engagement with Everyday Life* by Mihaly Csikszentmihalyi. He points out that our happiest times are when we are fully engaged in what we're doing, and when what we are doing is interesting and meaningful to us. (So maybe the hamster is experiencing pure joy as he runs?)

Mihaly writes on page 106: "The more responsibilities one has, the more essential it becomes to know what is truly important and what is not. Successful people often make lists, and quickly decide which tasks they can delegate, or forget about, and which ones they have to tackle personally, and in what order."

His book gave me the idea to list things I want to do. What a concept! Not just things I have to do, but things I want to do. Things that make me feel like my schedule is my own. My typical day's To Do list looks just like yours, I'll bet. Groceries, pick up dry cleaning, two hundred projects at work, after school this and that. It's all fairly common. But I try to add something else, something I like. If only one thing.

This month I added, to my own very great surprise, salsa-dancing classes. I even managed to sell two friends on the idea. The teacher is terrific, and perhaps best of all, one of my friends brings her kid, and the girls have a play date in the corner of the classroom.

I'm probably never going to salsa dance on stage with Julio Iglesias. I might not even go out salsa dancing once I graduate in ten weeks. That's not the point. I *look forward* to salsa-dancing class. I get excited about it. I think about the steps when I'm not at class. I imagine how much fun it will be when I get there. I talk to my daughter about how much fun she has playing with her friend. I make it happen! For that brief hour once a week, I'm not on the hamster wheel. I'm doing something that adds color and fun to my life. I find myself rejuvenated the following day. Ready to take on another week of similar tasks because I have found a moment when things are different. I've added a little salsa to a bland week, and found I like the taste very much.

What could you add to your life that may not be life altering, like going back to college or spending a month at a dude ranch in Wyoming, but that would add a little spice to your week? Start small and work up to Wyoming! You deserve it; put it on your list and see what happens.

The Collection

*I don't have a bank account, because I don't know my
mother's maiden name. —Paula Poundstone, comedian*

*I take my children everywhere, but they always find their way
back home. —Robert Orben, comedy writer*

When I was four, we lived with my great-grandpa in
Chicago in a creaky old house he had built before the
Depression. At night, I could see the lights from the alley
leaking in between the slats of the old venetian blind. It
made stripes on the bedspread in the bedroom my mom and
I shared. My great-grandpa, whom we called Pa, was giving
us refuge after my mom's divorce.

I remember the sound of trains. I remember how cold the
old, faded linoleum felt under my feet. I remember the
smell of very old carpet in Pa's bathroom. I remember the
china tea service that was ancient and that I couldn't
touch. It was painted in green and gold, with little pictures
of people in seventeenth century clothes and powdered
wigs sitting having tea.

I also remember making a picture of a locomotive engine
at school. We wrapped colored tissue paper around the ends
of pencils and used as much glue as possible to stick it onto
bright red construction paper. We glued on black paper
wheels. The teacher wrote my name in big block letters
across the bottom. I remember my mom being proud of it,
and she hung it on the wall above our bed. I remember

falling asleep in the big bed thinking about how my mom said that I was a good artist after seeing that train.

I remember these things because I know where the train picture I made thirty-two years ago is today. It is in a box carefully labeled WENDY, again in block letters, somewhere in my mother's house. My mom kept it. She kept a lot of things I made, or wrote, or drew. It's a pretty big box. If I were to sift through it, I would see the development of a child into an adult. She keeps other things, too. Now on her bookshelf she has many of the books I've written. She has all the little gifts and trinkets my brothers and I send to her.

It always made me feel proud that she kept some of my school stuff. I felt happy that she would hang it on the refrigerator, and that eventually, some of my work would end up in the box with my name on it. My brothers each have their own box, too. It comforted me to know that someone was tracking my progress. That someone was interested in what I was doing.

I have a box labeled SOPHIA, for my daughter. In it, we have pictures made with glued-on pinto beans and the mandatory kindergarten macaroni necklace. We have a math page where $9 + 7 = 20$. She's too young now to really understand the value of my collection. I read our job as parents is to give our children roots and wings. I have a box of roots in Chicago. My daughter has a box of roots in my bedroom closet in Malibu.

Someday, she'll look at the box and feel comforted to know her childhood has been preserved. She'll have memories to share, as will I, about the various projects and graded homework and math questions and smiley faces she brought home.

Like my mom, someday I'll suggest she take the box to her home, to enjoy. And if she's like me, she'll insist I keep it instead, no matter how much space it takes up. Because roots in mom's closet are safe, secure, comforting, and strong.

Finding Your Creative Spirit

Play an accordion, go to jail! That's the law!
—Bumper sticker

You call this a script? Give me a couple of $5,000-per-week
writers and I'll write it myself!
—Joe Pasternak, movie producer

Somehow the world got confused. It decided that creative people do things like paint or write or sculpt. It determined that True Creativity is the realm of artistes, like Martha Stewart or Danielle Steele. Well, here's a surprise: that's wrong information.

You have creativity oozing out of you, even if it's leaking on the floor. Parenting is, to my mind, true creativity. Remember when the baby was crying for no apparent or logical reason? Wasn't hungry or cold, the diaper tape wasn't sticking to her skin, nothing was wrong whatsoever. You came up with a solution, a way to help the baby stop crying. Years later, you artfully diverted your two-year-old from having a tantrum in the middle of the store. Tell me that doesn't require extreme creativity!

The Halloween costume you invented out of stuff you had around the house was a creation. The dreary winter day you and your kid cut snowflakes out of pieces of paper—that showed creativity. The way you juggle absolutely everything in your life, without much help at all; boy, oh, boy. That is creativity!

Women are perennially creative. I read a *National Geographic* article recently about the dirt-poor women of Rana Tharu. ("Rana Tharu: Women of Grace," *National Geographic Magazine,* December 2000). It had incredible pictures of them working, doing critical things like making portable stoves out of cow dung. (Who thought of that?) It also had pictures of them wearing the most exquisite colorful clothing, which they had made themselves. The creativity in those garments was astonishing. They had also made pots, all beautifully decorated.

Decorations mean nothing; they do not improve the functionality of anything. So why do these women spend their precious time, time they could spend washing clothes in the river or beating wheat stalks to reap grain, decorating pots and making their clothes beautiful?

Since the dawn of time, since the first humans, before there was language, there was art. Women and men have been creative since the beginning, crafting not only useful objects, but also cave art and embroidered garments and colored fabrics.

Art is part of our genetics. It isn't reserved for the style editors of *House Beautiful.* It's open to you, accessible to you, even if you have "no time" or "no energy." We stop our own creative flow by denying it, by pushing it aside, by trying to cast it off. We refuse to let our creativity flow through us. Entire books are written for artistic people about removing creative blocks of all kinds.

Maybe it's been a while since you indulged your creative side. For most women, this skill, or natural talent, is a delight to exercise. But sometimes we lose it along the path. I want my child to indulge in the joys of creativity, and I have always had a love of small handicrafts. We set up Thursday evenings as "Family Night" and our mutual favorite activity is doing an interesting craft project together. I get them from a hobby store, and I have a stockpile of ribbons and glue and construction paper and fabric scraps around all the time. We spend an hour or so making something. We've made Barbie clothes, crocheted, done paint-by-numbers, made ceramics, Christmas ornaments, grandparent gifts, and many other things. It's a great way to get in touch with my own creativity again, and to spend time delighting in my child's emerging sense of inventiveness.

You don't have to be Martha Stewart or Martha Campbell Pullen to make something and enjoy the process. Just choose something, anything—baking, rearranging furniture, crafts, the list is limitless—and let your creativity out of the box. Soon you'll see it spreading to other areas of your life and making your life as sparkly as, well, as sparkly as the glitter glue we accidentally got on the dog's tail last week!

Loving Your Body

I asked the clothing store clerk if she had anything to make me look thinner, and she said, "How about a week in Bangladesh?"—Roseanne Barr, comedian

In two decades, I've lost a total of 789 pounds. I should be hanging from a charm bracelet.
—Erma Bombeck, comedian, writer

I once read that when a man looks in a mirror, he admires all his good points, even if they exist only in his mind. But when a woman looks in a mirror, she sees only her flaws— and every detail of them.

Have you ever noticed that the ugliest, swarthiest man doesn't see the fact that he needs a shave, a bath, and to trim his nose and ear hair? Or to lose fifteen pounds? Nope, it seems men get an A+ in ignoring the things they don't like about themselves. We've all met guys who really need to look in the mirror.

Sometimes my mother looks back at me in the mirror. Or my grandma. Sometimes an old, worn-out hag who feels like she hasn't slept in a week stands there. Other times, I see the woman who needs to lose fifteen pounds. Occasionally, I see a reasonably pretty woman, but there's that one little flaw, or the tooth that's slightly turned, or the strand of hair that just isn't going the right direction.

I talked with some friends about this, and they agree. There are times when we think we're pretty, and times when we think we're not. It seems to be a universal female experience, like not having anything to wear although our closet is full of clothes. When we were teens, my friend's mother called it having "The Uglies."

I'm not much of a fashion plate. I don't read *Vogue* very often, unless I'm stuck somewhere and it is all there is to read. I cannot tell you what Madonna wore to the Oscars or who designed Cher's last dress. But I have learned one thing through observation and experimentation: We all have beautiful parts of ourselves to accent.

In the sometimes-exhausted world of single mother-hood, take a moment to stare at your face and body, stark naked, in the mirror some night. Do you have pretty feet? A nice nose? Soft, luxurious hair? What have the men you've dated complimented you on most often? What did your mom tell you was your best feature? What does your child or your best friend think is your best feature? What do *you* think is your best feature? There are probably several things you forgot you like about your physical appearance.

Next time you have The Uglies, decorate that best feature. If you have lovely hair, spend an extra ten minutes making it look really nice some morning. If you have perfect high cheekbones, get a book from the library on the proper application of blush, and experiment to make your-self look your absolute best. Buy some indulgent hand lotion and smooth it on your lovely feet before you go to bed tonight. Take a moment to be grateful for what's good about you before you set off for work in the morning.

Remember that old story about "I felt bad I had no shoes until I met a man who had no feet?" Be thankful for what's pretty about yourself, and watch your confidence, demeanor, and happiness soar. Don't beat yourself up in front of the mirror this week—celebrate what's lovely about you. You'll not only beat The Uglies, you'll start to reconnect with your feminine soul again. As we mother our children, we sometimes starve ourselves of compliments while feeding that energy to our children. Compliment and appreciate yourself today, and just see if it doesn't transform the rest of your day.

Just Say No in Minneapolis

I've tried several varieties of sex. The conventional position makes me claustrophobic and the others give me a stiff neck or lockjaw. —Tallulah Bankhead, actor

I'm too shy to express my sexual needs except over the phone to people I don't know.
—Gary Shandling, former comedy show host

Today I was at the post office and my neighbor Stu was just ahead of me in line. He's a particularly not-handsome man, with a questionable personality to boot. He's mean spirited in a curious, imbalanced sort of way, a cross between Scrooge and Elmer Fudd. He often wears clothes that look rumpled. Yet he considers himself to be quite a Don Juan, even though in all the time I've known him, he hasn't once been in a relationship—not even a one-night stand, as far as I know.

In line, however, he was flirting outrageously with a pretty blond woman who was sporting a large diamond ring on her left hand. He was being very complimentary and I guessed she was being merciful because he's so homely, or else she was completely oblivious to the fact that he was actually trying to seduce her.

His behavior annoys me intensely, and I've seen him do this before with other women. He reminds me of a man I met once at a street fair in Minneapolis. It was raining, pouring actually, and since I had jet lag anyway, I wandered from my hotel to see what all the people on the next street over were doing. I heard music. Thousands of people were hiding under eaves and umbrellas but still enjoying the evening's entertainment. There was music and food and junk vendors all over the rainy streets. A young man, perhaps college age, walked up to me and said, "Hello. Will you have sex with me?"

I was shocked, of course, and said no quite curtly. The people I was sharing an eave with laughed as the young man walked up to the next woman, huddled under an umbrella with a man she was obviously dating, and asked her the same question. When both of us turned him down, he went up to the next woman.

The mid-forties men next to me laughed when I questioned his behavior aloud. "Statistics!" one said. "Eventually, some woman will say 'Yes' tonight."

Although I despise his behavior, I have to admire the guy's persistence. He's probably made a fortune as one of those annoying telemarketers since then! He has to have a heck of a lot of confidence to repeatedly take rejection like that and keep on going.

Back in the post office with Stu and the blond, I have a strong feeling he doesn't see himself the way other people see him. Although I'm quick to criticize him for the many attempts he makes at getting a woman, any woman, to pay attention to him, this afternoon it hit me: Stu and the man in Minneapolis have a pretty high awareness of the laws of probability.

They are willing to try, over and over and over if necessary, to get what they want. They don't stop when they get no for an answer; they go right on to the next case. Now women largely shiver when we hear about men like this, and we wonder about the girls who may take them up on their all-too-blatant offers. We warn our daughters to stay away.

But when's the last time you wanted something, anything, so bad you wouldn't take no for an answer? When's the last time you dug in and got the raise you wanted? Got a scholarship so you could go back to school? Pursued a nice man who smiled at you and your child in the grocery store? When's the last time you set your heart on getting something, and then dedicated yourself to getting it, relying on the law of probability to deliver it to you in its own good time?

Less Is More Toast

She was so wild that when she made French toast, she got her tongue caught in the toaster.
—Rodney Dangerfield, *comedian*

Glamour is what makes a man ask for your telephone number. But it is also what makes a woman ask for the name of your dressmaker. —Lily Daché, *fashion designer*

When I was a little girl, I remember our minister insisting that everyone should buy the highest quality clothing and goods possible, and always travel first class because that's where you made important contacts.

I remember someone suggesting it was easy for him to say, but we didn't have two nickels to rub together. I learned through a typical American childhood that more is more and less is less. I learned that if you can have two pairs of cheap jeans, you are better off than having only one expensive pair. I learned that when it comes to shoes, why buy nice ones when you're going to wear them out someday anyway? I learned that it's almost sinful to buy something that isn't on closeout at the end of the season.

As an adult, I learned that spending money I didn't have for things I needed because they were on sale is the way to live. I learned that it's okay to buy lots of cheaper things. For instance, when the toaster I kept in my divorce finally broke after two years, I went out and looked. My goodness! Toasters can cost anything from $12 to $120 now. I "wisely" bought the cheap one—$12. Last week, it broke. It was about a year old. It came at the perfect time.

That same week, I was weeding out my closet as the season changed to cold weather. I had read a great idea last spring about putting a sticker on the front of all your clothes, so I'd taken a roll of old address label stickers and put one on the front of every item in my closet. Now that the season had changed, I took out all the clothes that should have been worn during the season just ended, but weren't. Anything that still had a sticker on had not been worn at all this past summer. So I put them into a pile for the Disabled American Vets to pick up.

As I sat down beside the pile when I'd finished, I began removing things from hangers and folding them into a box.

"Oh, yeah. I never liked this anyway," I thought, as I folded a blue shirt."

"This I got on sale—two sizes too big. Despite my poor attempt at alterations, these pants never fit right."

"I bought this in a hurry. It's an awful color on me every-where except under that store's lights."

"This was out of style by a decade when I bought it. What was I thinking?"

I added up what I remembered paying for the garments I gave away, many of which I'd worn only once or twice. Hundreds of dollars were about to be given away because of impulse buys, or buying something because it was on sale or was cheap and I needed one.

It got me to thinking about what that minister said, and now I think I get it. I have a few timeless outfits I truly love, that I bought carefully and spent real money on. (Okay, I got a few of them on sale, but they were still high quality.)

I love the color, the fit, the style, the fabric, and I know I look good when I wear them. That's money well spent, because those are the things I wear. The other stuff just fills my closet.

I think he was trying to tell us that to own a few good things is better than to own a lot of junk you never wear. I went shopping for a new sweater, just one, this winter. I'm wearing it now as I write this story. It cost me as much as I'd have felt comfortable paying for two or maybe three sweaters last season. But this one looks great on me, like someone designed it just for me. I feel great when I wear it, and truth be told, I've worn it a dozen times in the last month and I'm not a bit sick of it. I keep finding new things to wear it with, and it is a source of delight to me. In the long run, I will have saved money, because this sweater will get more use and will last longer because it is better made.

My daughter has a friend with a closet the size of her bedroom. The child must have forty or fifty different outfits and twenty pairs of shoes at any given time, bought by her indulgent mamma and her overworked dad. The outfits all come from fancy stores, some from Beverly Hills boutiques. The child generally wears her one or two favorites.

I used to buy my daughter a handful of new clothes every time we went out. Then I realized that she didn't wear what I bought; she only wears what she picks out. I experimented. She picked out two pairs of pants, one from a common department store, the other from a name-brand store for three times the price. She has no awareness of the dollar value of either pair. I watched silently. She wears the more expensive pair more than twice as often. She calls them her favorite pants. The cheaper ones not only don't get worn as much, the few times they have been worn the seam started to come undone. I cut our clothing budget by a third last year. We wear fewer better-quality clothes than ever before. It's remarkable how much better we feel about our images.

Oh yes—the new toaster works great, too. It should, for $45. And it comes with a three-year guarantee. Quality is more affordable than junk. Try it.

Homework Wars

There was a time when we expected nothing of children but obedience, as opposed to the present, when we expect everything of them but obedience. —Anatole Broyard, *author*

A good education is usually harmful to a dancer. A good calf is better than a good head. —Agnes de Mille, *dancer, writer*

In the terrific book *How to Motivate Your Child from Crayons to Career*, author Cheri Fuller tells the story of a group of failing students and frustrated parents who appeared on TV. She says they had so burned out on homework hassles that they were on national TV talking about their failure as parents.

"I tried everything!" one mother cried. "I grounded him, I took away his bike, I threatened. " The mothers had had it with the Homework Wars and were ready to surrender.

The kids apparently had had it, too. My third grader and I have now ended the Homework Wars, after a long year of second grade battles. Call me naive, but I had no idea that I would be doing an hour of second grade homework every night at my age. I had no idea that one day I would have to return to making things of glue and construction paper. No one ever told me that someday I would be in front of my kid trying to explain the principle of "carrying the one" to someone who would rather be playing Barbies.

I was singularly unprepared for the Homework Wars.

In the midst of my frustration, and not prepared to do third grade the same way we did second, I got a bunch of books on managing homework, the best of which seems to be Fuller's. I have read a half dozen of these books now, and I am glad to say they all have some common denominators, and that applying them worked in my house.

First, they all seem to talk about positive reinforcement, which means making homework enjoyable, not punishment. If this seems laughable, as it did to me six weeks ago, let me explain. We need to set up a specific area to do the homework in, somewhere other than in front of the TV or looking out the window. We use the kitchen table.

Then we need to make it an important time of day. They all say either give the kid some time to unwind after school and then bring on homework time, or else make it happen right away, depending on the child's personality. I have a snack-and-relax-for-a-while kid. She's tired out from school and needs a little break. I learned to make sure I spend at least five minutes of focused attention on her before she begins, so the whining that sometimes follows is not really a cry for attention.

Doing homework at a specific time each day is another piece of advice we've had success with. If you break and snack first and then begin homework at 5:30, then always begin at 5:30. Motivate your child to finish by cooking dinner while the homework is being completed. Dinner when you're done is a powerful motivator at my house now.

We also got over helplessness using their advice. I heard "My teacher never explained this!" several times. So I called the teacher and discovered that he was explaining it, it just wasn't sinking in. I told him I would support him in the classroom and he could support me at home by ensuring that they all got it. I told my child that I expected her to ask him for help at school and that she could ask me too. I raised my expectations and told her I would answer specific questions, not the general whine, "This is too hard!" I also said I would call the teacher and ask him why he hadn't explained the homework next time. I suspect this was a powerful motivator.

Now maybe my kid is easy to train because she's only eight, but so far, it's been working like a charm. I cannot tell you how much less stressful it makes evenings when I know that homework is one less battle I will need to wage in my own household.

Small Moments

Laugh and the world laughs with you,
Weep, and you weep alone
For the sad old earth must borrow its mirth
But has trouble enough of its own.
—Ella Wheeler Wilcox, poet

Grief is so selfish. —Mary Elizabeth Braddon, English writer

It's easy to forget how precious our moments with our children really are. It's easy to get so busy being a grownup with grownup things to do, all by ourselves as single moms, that we forget to share in the enthusiasm our children have for kittens and snowmen and butterflies and new crayons.

Of all people, I should know better. I should know to cherish each day with my daughter, to savor each moment we have together, to not expect her to be mature at eight, but to revel in her childishness and the beauty of her discoveries.

You see, Sophia is my third child. Long before she was even thought of, her father and I were on vacation in England with her older brother and sister. My son, Jeremy, was just over four years old and his baby sister, Amelia, had just turned eighteen months. We were enjoying a day of sightseeing when a car hit us at nearly seventy miles per hour.

Both of the children died in the crash.

I was gruesomely injured and very nearly died, too. I laid in a hospital bed for months and months waiting to learn to walk again and grieving my children. I swore that if I ever had another child, I would cherish every moment, that I would never take anything for granted again. I would never raise my voice, I would be the perfect mother, I would, I would, I would.

Sophia was born about two years later. I was on crutches for part of the pregnancy, but mostly physically recovered. She brought such joy into our lives! I was so delighted with this perfect little girl. We named her Sophia, which means "wisdom" in Greek, because we wanted to have gained wisdom from our ordeal, and gave her the middle name of Rose partly because of a scripture in the bible that promises the "desert shall blossom like a rose." Our hearts had become deserts.

I divorced her dad two years later. Mired in my own problems, emotional, financial, physical and other, little Sophia sometimes got lost in the shuffle. Sometimes, I forget that each moment is precious. Sometimes, I forget for a moment that she could die today or tomorrow. I forget the gaping loneliness I felt after losing her brother and sister a decade ago.

You'd think I'd never forget something like that, wouldn't you? You'd think I of all mothers would spend every moment being joyful for what I have now, grateful and happy.

A person could really beat themselves up over the slightest unkind word spoken to a child born after such a tragedy. Or really berate themselves over the time she was too tired to read one more bedtime story.

I do berate myself sometimes. I do wish I could constantly keep in mind the preciousness of my child's life and the awareness that, one day she will move away and be gone from me.

But it's human nature to not enjoy every moment. It's human nature to have bad days. It's human nature to forget. There's no excuse for being sharp-tongued with a child. There's no excuse for being too tired to be fully present with a child. But it still happens to all of us. I still make mistakes, and I still have to tell her I'm sorry.

I add this story to the book to comfort you. To remind you of two things: that your child's life is precious, but you already knew that. But also that you are human, and if parenting is hard, single parenting can be harder. I know you are being as good a mom as you can be. I know you are trying every day to be a better mom than you were yesterday. I know you focus on bringing your child joy, not just fulfilling his or her physical needs. And that is enough. It is all you can do—your best. It's all any of us can do. Comfort yourself in the knowledge that you are doing your best, and that no matter what happens, you can rest in the knowledge that you did just that—your best.

Flow, Names that Cannot Be Pronounced Easily, and Doing Things You Hate to Do

Every morning I get up and look at the Forbes list of the richest people in America. If I'm not there, I go to work.
—Robert Orben, comedy writer

You may already be a loser!
—Form letter allegedly received by Rodney Dangerfield, comedian

There is a book that has wafted in an out of my consciousness for years now. It's written by a professor at the University of Chicago. It's nearly lyrical in its combination of logic and philosophy, healing the conundrums of existence.

The professor's name is Mihaly Csikszentmihalyi (CHICK-sent-me-high-ee), and the book that intrigues me is *Finding Flow*, which is basically about how to find inner peace, joy, and beauty in everyday life. He swamps his points a little in some professorial words, but overall, the book is fascinating reading and a real thought provoker.

The professor researched the great life researchers when he wrote his book. The writings of Maslow, Nietzsche, and others are explored as they relate to the professor's suggestion that human happiness derives from finding "flow," the experience of being fully engaged in what you are doing and being truly happy at it.

He summarizes the other great teachers by saying on page 139: "The quality of life is much improved if we learn to love what we have to do." Earlier in the book he points out that doing what we love and loving what we do is a major secret to finding flow. We learn that the simple distinction between "I want" and "I must" makes all the internal difference in the world.

Sure, we may hate doing dishes, but if we make it a game and clock our completion time, it becomes an entirely different task. When I have to wake up early to prepare my child for school, even though I was up late the night before trying to meet a deadline, I can grumble through the morning or I can be delighted that I chose to have this child, that I chose to live as a single parent, and that I choose to teach her to value her education by arriving at school promptly.

Our focus determines our reality. If we move the "I musts" in life into the "I want to" category, the entire practice of living begins to transform itself. Not we must clean the kitchen, scrub the toilet, and fold the laundry; rather we *want to* live in clean, comfortable surroundings. Not we must go to work each day; rather we want to provide a standard of living for ourselves and our child(ren) that welfare doesn't offer.

Seen through the lens of conscious, life-affirming choices, life starts looking better each minute, doesn't it? I must go to bed now—no, wait. I *want* to feel wide-awake and fresh in the morning for tomorrow's joyful tasks.

Simply redefining your responsibilities in your head makes you happier to handle them. I know some single women pine for a relationship with a man. But in our hearts we know that any additional relationships besides what we have with our children takes work and time. A relationship with another adult would require you to modify the time you are spending with your child, and would change the emotional tenor of that parent-child bond. Why not celebrate the joys of that bond now, rather than focusing on what we don't have at the moment?

I believe we are the luckiest parents of all because we can design and redesign our lives at any time; we have all the benefits of being single, and we have the joy of having our children around as companions and as objects of our love and affection. Many of my single friends who are not parents envy the fact that I at least have someone to talk to and care about each day, when all they have is a cat. It's all in how you look at it.

Life can be glorious or awful at any given moment for any of us. A lot of it has to do with how we control our minds and what we focus ourselves on. Make a list of what's great about your life, and read it every morning and every time you're feeling down. This seemingly simple task can infuse your life with real joy and remind you that the glass is always half full after all, especially for single moms.

Christmas Cookies

How to Raise Your IQ by Eating Gifted Children—*Book title by Lewis B. Frumkes, 1983, as quoted in* The 2,548 Best Things Anybody Ever Said *by Robert Byrne*

Most Texans think Hannukah is some sort of a duck call.
—Richard Lewis, actor

Traditions create a sense of rhythm and season in a person's life. After my marriage ended, I felt afloat. I had no traditions of my own, only "us" traditions.

Look around. There are seasonal holidays in every religious and belief system, but there are also birthday traditions. Some cultures celebrate agricultural traditions, birth, death, and other rites of passage. In our hodgepodge world, you can find someone with completely different traditions than the ones you grew up with.

Traditions tie people and cultures together. They make things feel safe, secure, like all is right with the world. I knew in my heart it would be important for my child to have some traditions in her life as she grew.

With my family thousands of miles away, my two-year-old and I stared into a long, blank space in front of us. Like a sheet of paper, I could write on her memory any traditions I wanted, any beliefs, any dreams.

With all that blank space, I sat down and thought about traditions I wanted to create for my child and myself. I didn't want to repeat the same things I had done with her father, because he was no longer there. I didn't necessarily want to do the things my parents had done. I had gone through a lot to create a new life for us, and I was going to create valued traditions to match.

I considered all the activities and traditions I had experienced as a kid or as a wife, all the things I'd seen friends do, all the things other parents I knew did with their kids, all the things I saw friends' parents do when I was young. I wrote them down and thought hard about ways they could be adapted to our lives.

My grandmother used to bake sugar cookies with me when I was small. My mom added the idea of frosting them. I added the idea of making it a Christmas tradition and giving some away to friends and family. Now, all through the year, my daughter finds cookie cutters to add to our collection or decorative sprinkles she wants to use in December.

My parents used to spend Friday nights as "Family Night" with my brothers and me. We'd play games, talk, and often eat a special meal. I've incorporated this idea, too, into our life. My daughter and I consider our Thursday night Family Night nearly sacred.

My stepdad took great pains to make me feel welcome in the home he and my mom shared. He is gifted at making things with his hands, and he spent many hours working on various intricate craft projects with me. I adored him for it and grew up to love crafts.

My daughter and I make a point of doing one craft project each Thursday night Family Night. No matter how busy I am, I always plan something in advance to make sure she learns something interesting that night. Last week, it was how to crochet. We got beautiful yarn, and I showed her some basic stitches. We talked and laughed and soon she seemed to have the hang of it. Five minutes later, her doily had become a long snake-like shape, and we laughed as we pulled it apart to find where it had gone wrong. The joy she gets from observing this simple tradition makes it worth whatever it takes to create these memories.

I know that, like those sugar cookies I remember making with my Grandma when I was seven years old, I have started valuable traditions that will be remembered as proof that my love for her is enduring and that home is a safe refuge to return to. Perhaps she'll make her own traditions for my grandchildren someday. I'll be interested to see which ones she picks.

You can invent your own traditions too. Think about all the traditions you've seen and experienced. Perhaps you have been exposed to ideas from other religious or ethnic groups. Perhaps a book at the library would expose you to other things people do. Pick and choose and adapt what you like for your family. You could be creating a legacy that will last many generations after you are gone.

I remember reading about "The Red Plate." A woman had a set of four red plates when she got married, but one by one they had all broken by the time her first child entered grade school. She came up with the idea of using this special plate at dinner to serve the person who was celebrating something or deserved to be rewarded. This person—adult or child—was served first, and on the red plate, so the rest of the family knew that this was a special occasion. What a cute idea!

Nobody said traditions cannot begin with you, for better or worse. Once, a newly wed woman was preparing a roast for the family in the presence of her mother-in-law. The bride carefully cut both ends off the roast and put it in the oven.

"Why do you cut off both ends first? Does it make it juicier?" her mother-in-law asked.

"Oh, I don't know. My mother always did it that way," the young woman responded.

Intrigued, the young woman called her mother and asked why she had always cut off the ends of the roast. "That's the way your grandma always did it," her mother replied.

They called the grandmother and asked her. Grandma thought about it for a few moments. "Ah!" she recalled, "it's because when I was a new bride, my only roasting pan was too small to hold the whole thing."

Good-Bye Happily Ever After

I am a marvelous housekeeper. Every time I leave a man,
I keep his house. —Zsa Zsa Gabor, actor

For more than a year after my divorce, that phrase at the end of seemingly every book I read to my daughter, every Disney movie, every romantic tale, irritated me terribly.

"Happily ever after—ha! That's a laugh!" was my reaction. I felt like a pot boiling over with anger—at myself, at my ex-husband, at my fate. He'd promised to always love me; we'd planned to buy a little cabin when we got old, near a lake, like *On Golden Pond*, and invite the kids out to spend time with us.

We promised one another we'd hold hands when we walked down the sidewalk with our cardigans on and our silver hair.

Now it was Over, and I wasn't just mad, I was furious and hurt. Forgetting I was the one who filed for divorce was easy sitting in my puddle of bitter tears. How dare he leave me! And with a little child to care for, too!

That was six years ago, and although I'm no expert on divorce, I've got lots of friends who've walked through it, both as the leaver and the leavee. Everybody seems to rage against the broken promises as they angrily burn a relationship's worth of love letters and promises, mementoes and souvenirs. I've seen it so many times that now, when a friend gets a divorce, I know what to expect.

The brilliant and famous grief researcher, Elisabeth Kübler-Ross, explored how people grieve. Whether you left or he did, you eventually grieve the loss of all the dreams you had of happily ever afters, even if you're proud to have finally found the courage to have slain the dragon of your relationship.

The stages are:

Denial
Anger
Bargaining
Depression
Acceptance

We bounce up and down, all around, and through these stages, finally settling into a time of acceptance. While you are grieving your own losses, your child(ren) are grieving theirs as well. The whole process requires intense patience with yourself and your offspring. The most important thing I've learned from grief is that it is an organic process, and if you just let it grow, without trying to stifle it by forcing yourself into a new relationship before you're ready or shoving yourself into a smile that doesn't fit, you will heal much, much faster.

Allow your children to cycle through their loss. What they are losing is much different from what you are losing. Permanent rifts occur in the grief process when someone tries to oppress the style or reasons for another's grief. Allow yourself and your children room to move through these stages in a manner natural and normal for each individual, according to his or her own internal nature.

One More Push

I hate all sports as rabidly as a person who likes sports hates common sense. —HL Mencken, author

We all have the strength to endure the misfortunes of others. —Guy La Rochefoucauld, French nobleman

In the very, very distant past, I taught weight lifting to pay my way through journalism school. Not a lifter myself, I studied muscle groups and technique and spent a month in training at the gym I worked for. I would teach new customers proper technique, and then stand above them to "spot" them, which means offer the slightest amount of physical help to make sure they don't drop the weights on their chest and crush their ribs or any such thing. Sometimes a burly, muscular man would be trapped under an enormous weight, and with the added strength of just my two index fingers he'd have the extra oomph to push the weight back up.

I was reminded of my curious work history recently when a man I was dating told me he could bench press two hundred and twenty-five pounds. A bench press is when a lifter lies on his back and lifts a steel rod with heavy balanced weights straight up above his or her chest and straight back down. They do it repeatedly to gain muscle mass. Two hundred and twenty-five pounds is pretty impressive for anyone, and the poor man I was sitting across from had no idea I had been a coach, so my next question embarrassed him.

"How many times?" I asked politely. Considering his body size, this weight was quite a feat, nearly superhuman. It was a good fifty pounds more than he probably weighed.

"Just once," he said sheepishly. "Then I lie there, crushed under the weight of the bar, whispering 'Help me! Help me!' to anyone passing by."

We laughed at his funny retelling of the story, but there's a lesson in it too.

As a single mom, I sometimes bite off way, way, way more than I can chew. Do you ever do that? I think I'm Supermom, and I volunteer for a dozen things, make promises to my child and myself, and wake up to find myself crushed one morning under the weight of the responsibilities I accepted. Heck, sometimes I feel crushed just by having to take out the trash, drive to school and art class afterward, remember to buy eggs, and make sure I finish a project at work, much less by the extra stuff I get myself into. Then, if one thing goes wrong, like a cold or an emergency trip to the vet, I am immobilized. I have shifted into overwhelm, where I move at light speed accomplishing nearly nothing.

But instead of whispering "Help me!" I used to figure there's no one to help me anyway, so I'll have to wriggle out of it by myself. What I need at times like this is a family of friends to help me out, and I need a better foreknowledge of my own strengths and limitations.

Somewhere after the invention of the automobile, Americans lost a sense of community. It still exists in some places, but the sense of community and helping one another comes from working and playing with other people, and we often don't have time for that anymore.

Friends are like a bank—we make deposits of love, help, and companionship, and we withdraw the same. If you overload yourself with responsibilities and take no time to truly consider your own limitations, chances are you'll be crushed under the weight. The answer isn't to give up weight lifting, or volunteering, or trying to get involved in your child's life or school. A big part of the answer is to build up your limits, build up friends who can help you if you overcommit yourself, and take the time to build up your mental and time management muscles so you can confidently accomplish all that you wish to do.

With a little help, you'll be able to give it one more push!

Secret Wishes

When you wish things were different than they seem, a friend is one who shares your dreams. —Tina Maxson, poet

Trust in Allah, but tie your camel. —Arabian proverb

Have you ever wished for something? Have any of your wishes ever come true? Was it what you hoped for when it came? We've all heard "Be careful what you wish for, you just might get it!" and we've listened to jokes and stories about genies popping out of lamps to grant three wishes to a rescuer.

I may be too fanciful for some people's taste, but one year at the after-Christmas sales I found a small round box. It was covered in royal blue velvet and decorated with shimmering gold sequins and elaborately scrolled gold braid. It was just what I needed.

I took it home and pulled out an old manila folder. I cut the folder into circles precisely the same size as the inside of the box. On them, I wrote a wish and the date I was making the wish, then I put each one in the box. I call it my "God Box" because I think of it as a place to store my prayers.

The box is very special, and until today when I wrote this, nobody even knew I had it. My daughter has seen it but never opened it. I have a policy about the God Box. Once a wish goes inside (and I do add to the box sometimes), I stop fretting about it. I trust that I am now focused on achieving that wish, and that magical or heavenly forces are waiting to help me fulfill it at the perfect time.

It might sound silly, but it's worked for me *and* it brings me peace of mind. In human history, people chose beliefs that empowered them and their community, so why not choose to believe in your own God Box, or if you prefer, "Wishing Box."

Want to hear about a wish that came true? It might inspire you to acquire a box for yourself. In 1997, my daughter and I were crammed into a tiny one-bedroom apartment, albeit in a beautiful location.

Before you think I'm complaining, I have to say this microscopic place was on the beach in Malibu. I'd moved there so my daughter could start kindergarten in a terrific school. I wanted to live in this miniature apartment until I found the perfect house. So I wrote on the wish card: "A house, a dog, and a lemon tree." I'd go out looking on Sundays at all the new listings in my price range. I looked at dozens and dozens of houses and condos, but none were right. I'd open the God Box, read the wish card, kiss it, and put it back in the box.

I kept driving by one house that wasn't for sale. Every time I passed it, I'd think, "Someday, I'll be able to afford a house like that one." Then my friend who lived right across the street from the fantasy house called to say it had just been put it up for sale. The price was $200,000 more than I could afford. I went to see it and spoke to the owner. I said, "If you don't sell it for any reason, please call me. I'll lease it, I'll take it with an option to buy, I'll make the terms work for both of us." Fat chance, but it was a beautiful house. I kept looking at others.

Through what amounts to nearly a miracle, the family who owned the house inherited a large sum of money and had a job offer out of the city that suddenly made them very motivated to leave. Three months later, almost exactly a year after I'd first seen it, I closed escrow on that house at a price I could afford. Six weeks later, we got a German shepherd puppy. But the most ironic thing was a housewarming gift from a friend. You guessed it—he brought a lemon tree tied with a bow!

I took the wish card out and wrote the completion date on it. I have older wishes in the box than the house, and newer ones too. But it comforts me to know that that little box hides in my bedside table. It's a joy to take a card out and write GRANTED across it in flowery purple ink. Looking at the granted wishes and the ones yet to come makes me feel excited, and in some ways reminds me of the times my ex-husband and I used to lay in the dark whispering our secret dreams for our future together. When my daughter is a little older, we will make a box for her, too, to put her secret wishes in.

Isn't it time you put a box next to your bed?

Starting Over, Again

You can no more win a war than you can win an earthquake. —Jeanette Rankin, first female member of the House of Representatives

If you have any problems at all, don't hesitate to shut up. —Robert Mankoff, humorist

Charlotte moved to America a few years ago with her ten-year-old son and several suitcases. I've never moved into or out of another country, so I asked her what it was like. "It was a wonderful chance to start over," she said. "We left all sorts of things we didn't really need—life's clutter—back in France." Charlotte has rebuilt her life and her son's here, thousands of miles from home. I think she's brave.

My old buddy Joel used to live in a wild canyon in the Santa Monica mountains. One year, a brush fire came and burned his house to the ground. He lost a lifetime of possessions and memories. He spoke about it: "It really made me see how little all the stuff we collect really matters. I didn't like it, but I got a fresh start."

Down the street in the blue two-story house with the nice yard, they had a garage sale last weekend. The woman who owns the house found her husband cheating again, and finally left him. The house they shared is now for sale, and she's moving into a small apartment with the two girls at the end of the month. Her life's goods were marked down cheap in her front yard. I ask her how she's doing. "I'm glad to have a chance to start my life over," she assures me.

All these people had to begin again, for very different reasons. Perhaps you can relate to starting over. Life seems to be a series of stops and starts. My life rarely crescendos, it stops with a slam! And then I pick up the pieces and begin again.

After so many years of this, I've come to simply accept the slams. I accept that whether I want it to happen or not, lots of things end. We choose to move, to leave a bad marriage, to have another child, to not have another child, lose a job, or change careers, and each time we choose, our life changes.

Each time our lives change, we have a chance to begin again. It's rather like looking at the four-foot-tall stack of dirty dishes in the kitchen. If you don't just dig in and start on them one at a time, it will never get done. The Dish Fairies have yet to show up at my house!

I suppose it is all in how we look at Starting Over. Is it an exciting fresh start, a chance to edit the script of our lives, or is it a horrid burden? How we spend the journey is how we live our lives. Which will you choose? Are you pleased that today is a new day to start over?

Finding Joy

I locked my keys in the car and had to break the window to get my wife out. —Red Skelton, *comedian*

There are days when it takes all you've got just to keep up with the losers. —Robert Orben, *comedy writer*

Several books ago, I was working with a Florida publisher. The nature of the book required me to call them often, and while it wasn't a huge operation as far as publishers go, there were perhaps a hundred employees.

The lady who answers the phone there is named Joy, coincidentally. Some people seem to be named what they are, because every time I called, this chirpy lady was glad to talk to me. Despite the hundreds of people who surely called in a day, she seemed to remember my name and to care that I actually got through to the person I was trying to reach.

Sometimes we talked of personal things. I learned a bit about her family, and I remember when she had to go back to her home state for a funeral. But mostly, she just had to quickly put my call through and move on to the next blinking light on her switchboard.

I guess the thing that impressed me most about Joy was that she seemed to take real joy in doing her job well. In this world of long, long phone lines everywhere you turn, and Press 1 to get nobody, it's a wonderful thing to meet someone who has to deal with the public all the time yet isn't irritable, bored, and trying to get out of as much work as possible and still get paid. We've all had to Press 2 for one option, only to Press 4 for another, and three buttons later discover we're going to be on hold for twenty minutes but that the company is really sorry. So sorry they'll fill our heads with nasty elevator music!

My job requires that I be nice to people all day. My daily routine requires that I be nice to the people at the post office where I mail my book manuscripts, and the people at the copy shop, the checkers at the grocery store, and the people at the gas station. When I'm promoting a book, I may get only a few hours of sleep a night when I'm on tour, and I still have to get up at 4:30 A.M. and be nice to a television station host. Some days, it feels like my whole life is customer service! Do you ever feel that way?

It's easy after a long day of being nice to forget customer service at home. I forget that my number one customer is only eight years old. I forget that reserving energy and love and politeness for the people I live with is my primary duty all day, whether or not I was nice to the gas station attendant and the grocery bagger.

I admit that once when my daughter forgot to set napkins on the table and then asked me to get them as I'd just sat down at last after a hard day and making dinner and helping with homework, I snapped, "Get it yourself!"

I also admit that I am a big believer in Joy. Joy the phone receptionist, and joy in my personal life. When I manage to be joyful and polite at home, the mood of my home life improves dramatically. When I'm grumpy and all out of joy, it plummets. I realize that I set the emotional tone for my household.

I've begun a new technique, and maybe it will work for you, too. Maybe it will help you bring a little more joy into your after work-after school life. It works for us. For five minutes, or ten if I can spare them, I sit in my car before I pick up my daughter. I take half a dozen deep breaths, releasing the annoyances of the day, and I picture my kid in my mind. I picture her laughing and happy. I think of how much she means to me and how much I love her. Somehow, the evenings just go more smoothly when I've reloaded my joy-o-meter.

Brave Heart

Boy, the things I do for England.
—Prince Charles, upon sampling snake meat

*I loathe people who keep dogs. They are cowards who haven't
got the guts to bite people themselves.*
—August Strindberg, German writer

We tend to think of courage as something that extraordinary people demonstrate under extraordinary circumstances. A fireman pulls a baby from a burning building. That's courage. A woman jumps into a freezing river to save her drowning child. That's courage. A farmer battles a raging storm to save his beasts. That's courage.

People said I had courage when I survived the terrible car crash that killed both my children. What I learned is that it wasn't a special kind of courage. Frankly, I don't think it's a special courage to save the baby, or your drowning child, or your livestock.

I think courage is something we all use, almost every day. Very few people live gilded lives with no worries, no matter what you read in *People* magazine or see on *Entertainment Tonight*. The city I live in, Malibu, has lots of stars, and I promise you one thing: they've got problems, too. Sometimes more than we do.

Courage to me is simply this: doing it again. Getting up with that alarm clock one more time and doing it again, every day, day in and day out. It's getting up to nurse a sick child five times in one night, even though you have to be at work by eight the next morning. It's going in to a job you wish you could leave so you can afford night classes. It's leaving a bad relationship and deciding to make a go of it on your own because that's what you believe is best for you and your child.

Courage is what single moms display every single day. Courage is being there for your child when you're tired and sick yourself. Courage is believing that right now is just fine and tomorrow's going to be even better. Courage doesn't require a dramatic situation where almost anyone with any sense would do the right thing, and often without thinking. Courage is the myriad good decisions you make that contribute to a child who will become a happy, healthy adult. Courage is being you, doing what you do to the best of your ability, every day, whether you feel like it or not. You're the heroine in your own story. Take a bow!

Sleeping Beauty

Hope is the feeling you have that the feeling you have isn't permanent. —Jean Kerr, writer

Goodnight Moon. Goodnight cow jumping over the moon. Goodnight light, and the red balloon. Goodnight bears. Goodnight chairs. —Margaret Wise Brown, author

Two weeks ago I participated in a poll on the Internet of people all over the world, because I wanted to see the statistics that resulted. They asked people how much sleep they need. The most popular option selected according to the survey was five to eight hours per night.

Then they asked how often people get that much sleep. The majority of people still said they get enough. I am guessing the majority of people surveyed were not moms!

I read an article on how prolonged depression is partly a result of not getting enough sleep. It depressed me just to think about it! How can we get enough sleep with the laundry to be folded, the house to tidy, toys to pick up, and, of course, we need time to relax!

I took an informal poll of my girlfriends, other mothers. "Do you think you get enough sleep?" I asked. Almost all of them said, "No, but I try to catch up on weekends," or "Sometimes, yes. But mostly not."

It seems such a simple thing, to get enough sleep. Being responsible for your entire household requires that you be functioning at peak levels. That means getting enough sleep most of the time.

Most women's sleep needs change during the month. Some of us need more sleep around our periods, and others need less. Have you paid attention to what your body needs? Do you listen to internal signals, or do you just push and push yourself to exhaustion?

Getting enough sleep makes you more efficient when you're awake. It can increase your patience with your child, make you prettier and more energetic, boost your immune system, give you the extra power to do those last few things you need to do. It can even increase your tolerance with your child's homework! Let a few things slide for a week or two while you catch up on your rest; you'll surprise yourself with the energy to complete them more easily later.

When we see our kids being grumpy, we know they probably are hungry or sleepy, and we act to alleviate their problem. Doing that same thing for ourselves, not just once in a while but over the course of months, can make you into a totally new and improved person. I can't tell you right now how I know this to be true—it's past my bedtime!

Sleep Softly and Carry a Big Stick

It was such a lovely day, I thought it was a pity to get up.
—Somerset Maugham, author

When my ex moved away, I was left in a big house with a small child and an even smaller dog. In those first months, everything that creaked, groaned, whizzed, or whined in the night was, I was sure, some burglar coming to kill us both. More than once, I raced to my daughter's room, locked her door with us inside, and dialed 9-1-1, I'm embarrassed to say. Usually, the very kind police arrived and noticed it was windy and there was a tree limb grown too close to a window, or there was a loose shingle flapping. I was, shall we say, a little skittish.

In addition to the nightly fears, spooky things happened. One day I decided to hammer something back into place, but the hammer was missing from the garage. It was not where I had left it, and since I was the only adult who ever came into the house, no one could have moved it accidentally. It was gone.

Once my diary was not where I had left it. Instead, it was half shoved under my bed, instead of being carefully stored in the night table. I don't believe in ghosts, but I was starting to wonder.

It was a huge adjustment to get used to being the only adult in a house at night, taking full responsibility for my own and my child's safety. Before, I'd had a strong husband who at least seemed to be there protecting me. I had known there was another adult I could rely on in an emergency. Now what would happen if I fell off a ladder while I changed a light bulb?

Eventually, I had frightened myself so many times that I got a security system. I didn't mention it to my ex, which was easy to avoid since we weren't talking then anyway.

That night, I set the alarm and put the dog in the unarmed part of the house. I put my child to sleep, and I laid down feeling secure for the first time in weeks.

Shortly after midnight, the alarm went off! I knew the system was automatically dialing the police for me, and feeling brave in that fact, I ran to the picture window looking over the huge back yard. I saw a man running, as fast as he could, out toward the gate!

Terrified, my heart thumping, I ran to the side of the house where I could see the street. I saw the would-be burglar as he jumped into his car and quickly turned. As it passed under the streetlight, I saw that it was a car I recognized. In fact, it was a car that had once parked in my garage—it was my ex-husband's!

The next day I called him and confronted him about his nocturnal visits. He denied having taken anything from the house, although later he admitted it. It turns out he had indeed visited in the night plenty of times, breaking into "his" house and apparently helping himself to anything he felt he was being deprived of, including access to my journal!

I kept the alarm system, and months later, a bird flew into the window and set it off and nearly scared me to death. I got a steel sword and a wooden billy club that had belonged to an ancestor and kept it next to my bed. I slept with my daughter in bed beside me on nights I felt particularly vulnerable. Soon I didn't hear the scary night noises any more. Eventually, I stopped noticing little scratching sounds or even things that go bump in the night.

After a while, I got used to being in charge of everything. I got used to being responsible for our safety. I got used to being cautious and careful. I felt mildly embarrassed about my prior fears until I talked to other single moms. It seems a lot of us go through the same thing—fearing for our children and ourselves when we are first alone again, no matter how long we were single before.

It may not seem like much of an accomplishment now, but we need to acknowledge our strength and bravery and our increased ability to cope. Whether we elected to be single parents or not, we've taken on a big responsibility and we all work hard at it.

Getting used to living alone again is easier, I believe, if you are not also responsible for the safety and well-being of your children. But you made it through this and the thousands of other adjustments you had to make to become the mom you are today. To get as far as you've gotten, you overcame your own fears, learned new skills, and conquered your inadequacies. Maybe you had to learn how to take care of a car, or how to make repairs to the house, or how to discipline a child or any other things that were "his" job when you were living with your child's father.

Take a moment and credit yourself for all you've done. Even if no one in your life is willing to give you a pat on the back for your arduous journey, give one to yourself. You deserve it!

Boarding School Blues

I tended to place my wife under a pedestal.
—Woody Allen, comedian

*I happened to catch my reflection the other day when I was
polishing my trophies and, gee, it's easy to see why women are
nuts about me.* —Tom Ryan, athlete

Laura was a happily married wife with a new baby, a new
house, and a decent job until she found out Chad was
cheating on her. The marriage ended shortly afterward, and
Laura was left an unhappy woman with a toddler, a slightly
used house, and a decent job.

All her life she had wanted to be a mom, to stay home
like her mother had done and raise a family, to do lunch
and get her nails done and go workout at the gym once the
kids were in school full time. She said, "It sounds simple,
but that was what I wanted from the time I was a little girl
playing with dolls. I always thought wives had it the best."
Now it was all on her shoulders, and it didn't feel so good.

After she got her sea legs as a single woman again, Laura
started dating. No sooner had she done so, though, than
she became alarmed by the number of men who not only
didn't want a woman with a young child, but didn't want
children at all.

"I went out with one man," she tells me over iced teas at
a popular coffee shop, "who said, 'I think it's great that you
have a kid.' He looked politely at her son Todd's picture.
"Do you want any more?" When she said yes, he said that
he did not, but she let it slide. He was such a nice man! He

made her feel so special, always focusing all his attention on her when they went out, buying her little gifts, flowers, dinners. It was very charming. He was also kind to her son when the three of them went to the zoo, even though the boy was only two and tired easily.

Laura was thinking she'd found the ideal man. Maybe he'd change his mind about having more kids once he got to know how wonderful her little angel already was. They got home from the zoo and put Todd down for his nap. The happy couple curled up on the couch. Her new man said, "I think it's really important that boys learn to be tough at an early age. My parents sent me away to school when I was ten. It was good for me."

Laura froze like a startled lizard. Her friend continued, "It's better for the parents, too, if the child isn't around. My parents were very busy people. Busy people can't have children and get anything done."

His mother and father were both successful, wealthy attorneys, and his father had eventually become a judge. Laura said, "I felt this cold air rush through my veins. He was hinting that he would like me to consider the same for my boy!"

I said, "Are you suggesting that I would want to send Todd away?" He looked at me and said, "Sweetie, not for a long, long time. He's just little right now. But someday, it would be good for him. Plus, then I'd have you all for myself. I don't want to share you with anyone."

Laura practically recoiled from him. "This is my child," she said, "not something I want to put away. I had him because I want him with me." She broke up with that man shortly thereafter. "I never knew how important that one little question is," Laura says now. "Now I know if they say they don't want kids they probably mean it, so that's my exit line. I think men who don't want children really shouldn't date women who already have them."

Tick, Tock, Biological Clock

I knew I was an unwanted baby when I saw that my bath toys were a toaster and a radio. —Joan Rivers, comedian

Marriage is a great institution, but I'm not ready for an institution. —Mae West, early feminist icon

Yvonne wanted another baby. She loved their soft, fuzzy heads and the smell of baby powder. She loved it when they cooed and kicked their little legs in freedom when their diapers were changed. She liked everything about babies, especially how dependent they are on their mothers. It made her proud to push a stroller, and count each new tooth, and record each milestone in their baby books.

She knew what she was talking about when it came to babies, too. When I first met her, she had a three-year-old and a five-year-old whose daddy was long gone and never heard from. I'd say to myself that's a lot of work, but Yvonne didn't feel that way. She wanted a husband and with him, another baby.

"It's my biological clock," she insisted when I told her she might not need another baby. What do I know?

A year or two went by, and we swapped stories and baby-sitting duties and shared a few kids' birthday parties. We pushed swings together at the park, and Yvonne stuck to her plan: find a man, get pregnant, have another baby.

Just one more would satisfy her, she assured the park mommas and me.

I moved away from that town and lost touch with a lot of friends. Near Christmas, I called Yvonne. She told me she was seven months pregnant! I congratulated her on her goal, and she assured me she was delighted. I asked her about the father. Well, he wasn't around any more; he'd been a short relationship, and she told me she'd practically begged him to get her pregnant. He'd apparently obliged. She'd never meant him to be marriage material.

Now it was her and the kids, and she had an aunt an hour or so away who would be coming over to help when the new baby was born. I felt surprised by the news, and also admired her. The baby had been her goal, not a relationship, and whether or not anyone thinks it is moral or right, she'd achieved it.

I sent a gift when her daughter was born, and called now and then. Life was hectic, but she was coping, and much to my surprise, she was happy. Alone, with three kids and a full-time job as a paralegal, but she was making it work. The children are happy, well fed, and cared for. The older two are in school now, and her life is intensely busy, but she got that third baby. Who among us is qualified to judge her choice?

I Like Myself!
I Like Myself!

The last time I saw him he was walking down lover's lane holding his own hand. —Fred Allen, writer

About three hundred people were crowding into the vast cavern of an auditorium. It was early evening, and some of us were wearing business suits from the long day just passing. Others came from home, apparently, in jeans or casual clothes. It was a festivity of colors and the peculiarly lovely sound of a room full of people holding a hundred, perhaps a thousand, different conversations at the same time.

The lights on the high ceiling twinkled down on us. The expansive stage was set with long royal blue drapes and two bold floral arrangements on either end. It was indeed a special event, and each one of us had paid hundreds of dollars to be here.

Finally, the announcer came out and stood at the shiny stalk of a microphone. We all rushed to our seats and focused expectantly on the platform. He introduced the speaker, and as that man walked out from behind the curtain, the room reverberated with applause.

The tall, thin man we'd all come to hear walked up to the microphone smiling. He was perfectly dressed in a tailor-made dark blue suit, every hair in place, and a fat, expensive watch glinting off his lean wrist. He smiled a broad smile at the crowd and began speaking.

We listened, enraptured by his words and enlivened by his ideas. He talked to us about *self-esteem*, which is learning to love yourself. He told us that without self-esteem we make poor life choices, poor relationship choices, and poor career choices.

As he talked, it became clear that self-esteem is very important to our emotional well-being. He told us stories of people without self-esteem and how it negatively affects their lives. He shared anecdotes about people who built up their self-esteem and transformed and their lives. He told us about research that indicated that people with high self-esteem do better in life, are less depressed, describe themselves as happier more often, are more resistant to being taken advantage of, and gain many other benefits.

Eager now for one drop of the precious tonic of self-esteem, I sat forward in my seat, pen poised. He offered a technique: "Stand in front of your mirror for ten minutes each day, telling yourself, 'I like myself! I like myself!' over and over, with gusto and feeling."

He offered several other techniques too, but this is the one that most struck me. I'm the kind of person who gains self-esteem from accomplishments. I feel best about myself when I have done something I can be proud of, whether it is giving the vagrant on the corner $2 or closing a huge business deal. The speaker's rousing and helpful chat got me thinking, so I asked my friends what made them feel most confident and gave them the highest self-esteem. Ask yourself these same questions and see if it doesn't helps you too.

What makes me feel confident?

What boosts my self-esteem?

What makes me feel self-motivated?

My friends' answers were:

Having a good relationship with others.

Being proud of my career accomplishments.

Feeling emotionally connected to my child.

Living up to my own moral standard.

Doing what I planned to do.

Achieving goals I set for myself.

Getting recognition from others.

Having integrity in what I say.

Looking good and feeling healthy.

Feeling like I am in charge of my life.

Their answers made me think. Besides the interesting idea of standing in front of a mirror, what other ways will help us feel better when we are feeling down? For me, dressing better than I feel seems to work for minor blues. Here's a technique that builds overall self-esteem for a lot of people:

At night, take out your journal and write down a few good things, happy things, reasons you are proud of yourself. Benjamin Franklin wrote about this technique in his autobiography. I found it there and have used it successfully myself. Write down how close you came to being the kind of person you wanted to be today. What did you do that you wanted to do, how well did you live today? Compliment yourself on the things you did well, in writing. It's remarkable how transformative building a "confidence journal" can be. (And, of course, the next morning you can always read it aloud to yourself in front of the mirror!)

Yellow Cab

What do we live for, if not to make the world less difficult for each other?—George Eliot, author

If all the cars in the United States were placed end to end, it would probably be Labor Day weekend.
—Doug Larson, writer

I saw Barbara in the school parking lot yesterday along with her toddler, who travels everywhere with her. She shuttles her elderly mom to doctor's appointments, her middle school-aged daughter has four nights of after-school activities, and her fourth-grade son has three nights of different after-school activities. She and her seventy-work-hours-a-week husband have to travel twenty-six miles round-trip from their house to her daughter's school, dropping her son off in between. She often tells me how exhausted she is from being a cab driver for her family.

Jane lives closer to school. She and her husband, Carl, and their also-fourth-grade son live a few miles from me. They have two luxury cars, a big house, and although her husband works full time, she does not. She has cleaning help to pick up after the family and the Pekingnese twice a week.

Jane is a beautiful woman, enhanced by days spent going from one exercise class to the next, getting nails and hair done, and generally investing vast amounts of time in perfecting her already perfect face and body. She drives her child the six miles to school and then goes off to her appointment for the day, stopping to lunch with a friend before returning to pick up her child, who does ten weeks of sports in the fall and no other after-school activities that I know. She, too, often complains about how exhausted she is from being the cab driver for her family.

Across town, in a large home on the beach, is a semi-mansion. Corinne has two children, both in the same school but with very different after-school interests. Corinne's husband works full time, and she probably has a cleaning lady too, although I've never asked her. I've never asked her because I've rarely seen her standing still. She is constantly volunteering or recruiting volunteers, calling or collecting, helping at the school, getting involved in civic matters, and so on. She has a Ph.D. from her pre-mom days, and is very active in her husband's business. Once, our daughters were in the same art class after school. I was telling her that I needed to go out of town but was having trouble finding a nanny for three days. She immediately volunteered to watch my child! I declined, but you know what? I've never heard her complain about how exhausted she is from being the cab driver for her family.

Then there's Georgia. She and her daughter live alone in a small apartment in a dingy building. Georgia always manages to bake cookies for the class party. She shows up at the school to have lunch in the cafeteria with her daughter. She runs a small business but somehow manages to remember to take her kid to the park and to all her after-school activities. Absolutely everyone in town knows who she is, either because she's helped them or spent social time with them. She moves at the speed of light, just like Corinne above. And I've never once, ever, heard her complain about how exhausted she is from being the cab driver for her family.

These are four really different women, with really different lives. But one thing is the same: each of them gets twenty-four hours a day to live. For probably around eight of those hours, they each lie in a warm, soft bed. So what makes the difference between the ones who complain and the ones who do not? It occurs to me it might be their attitude. It must have been an example like this that led someone to say, "If you want something done, give the task to a busy person." While the kids are small, why not choose to relish the many duties and the crushing schedule? Soon they'll be asking for our car keys, and some day they will be driving off for good, never to live with us again. If I am exhausted or delighted by my tasks, I will experience either exhaustion or delight. I think, hmmm, let me see. I think I'll choose delight today.

Dealing with Dear Old Dad

He never found her, though he looked
Everywhere
And he asked at her mother's house
Was she there
Sudden and swift and light as that
The ties gave
And he learned of finalities
Besides the grave.
—*Robert Frost, from* The Hill Wife

Even though there are probably days when you wish he'd leave the planet, your children's dad is still part of their lives. I remember thinking I was going to get rid of my ex when I divorced him, only to discover now I had to be involved with him every single week, and I had to be nice if I wanted the whole custody thing to go smoothly. Yuck!

I know better than to say bad things about him in front of my child. Any psychologist will tell us that the parent who does the accusing loses the kid's affection faster than the parent who is being accused. So I keep my mouth shut, like most single moms do. But there are times I sure wish I could blow off some steam when he does something (still!) that annoys me or that I think is unfair to our child.

The matter of the ex is a touchy subject for most women. Here's this guy you left, or who was foolish enough to leave you, but by very fact of your child, you still have to deal with him, at least occasionally. I once sat next to an eleven-year-old boy traveling alone on a four-hour plane trip. He was carrying a gold fish bowl wrapped in plastic wrap. He was obviously upset. We got to talking. After I'd gotten the fish's name, Spot, we became buddies.

He told me, "At the end of the summer, I go back to my mom's house. I go to my dad's every summer."

I asked him if he liked it. "Well, I like my dad and his wife a lot. They have a cool house, and we do a lot of fun things. But I like my life with my mom, too. It just is really hard that in summer I have to leave all my friends and then come back and try to get it all back again."

I asked him if there was a solution. Would he prefer to live with just one parent and not see the other at all?

"No, I love them both. I wish my dad hadn't remarried so he and my mom could get married again, but they fought all the time. I sure remember that!"

He looked out the window and tried to compose himself. "It's just so hard on the kids when parents have to do this!" he said angrily. "It's just not fair!"

I let him sit with his anger for a while. Then I gently said, "What would make it better for real?"

"Nothing," he said sadly. "Nothing would make it better. I want to see them both. But I wish they would say nice things about the other one when I'm with them. " Then he told me stories of the nasty things his dad says about his mom when he gets there. He defended her to me.

Then he told me sadly that his mom would now make him throw away the clothes his dad bought him during the summer because she won't like them. And she'll complain about his father. "She might even make me throw away Spot!" he said, looking sadly into the fish bowl, "just because she doesn't like anything my dad does."

He sat in sulky eleven-year-old-boy silence, looking gloomily into the fish bowl. "Why can't they get along? I mean, that's why they got divorced. Why ruin my life?"

You know, it takes a big person to get along with a hateful ex-spouse for the sake of a child. It takes a mature adult to allow in some things we may not have chosen. Certainly if the ex is using substances or is violent or grossly uncouth and encourages by example or weakness such things in our child, there's every reason to stand up and even enlist the courts again in settling the matter. But for the twenty million other annoying things the ex does, perhaps for the child's sake it's better to just look the other way.

I remember remarking to my ex that we got along better now than we did when we were married. I try to ignore it when he semi-intentionally does things that annoy me. I very rarely say bad things around my daughter about her dad. I figure when she's old enough, she will make her own judgments about our respective behaviors.

Sometimes, I wonder what happened to that little boy and Spot. I wonder if his mom really did throw everything away and flush Spot down into a watery grave. Or did she realize that her boy's feelings were more important than her own anger, hurt, and vengeance?

If It Ain't Dirty, Don't Wash It

Housework can kill you if done right.
—Erma Bombeck, author

There is no need to do any housework at all. After the first four years, the dirt doesn't get any worse.
—Quentin Crisp, writer

My mom kept a perfect house, despite three kids and a German shepherd. At any given moment, you could just throw your dinner on the floor and eat off it, it was that clean. My mom dedicated huge amounts of time, and still does, to keeping an immaculate house.

As her only daughter, it was of course my responsibility when I was a teenager to show my mother how the other side lives. I made a point of keeping my room in such a state of disarray that if you threw your dinner on the floor, not only would you never find it again, but if you did, eating it would be lethal.

But as daughters do, when I grew up and had children of my own, I knew that keeping a clean, nearly immaculate, house was part of my destiny. So I tried, honestly. I tried hard. Two babies, a small dog, and a small business, but somehow, I never quite managed the hang of perfectly clean linoleum at the same time all the dishes were done.

Guilt became the name of the game, especially if mom was coming for a visit.

Then I got divorced. Now I had full responsibility for all the filth we created, *and* I had to earn a living *and* take out the trash *and* take the car in for service.

I became an investigator of ways to cut corners. Perhaps you've done this too. First, I acknowledged that however my mother had managed to do it, keeping a perfect house was not a gift I had inherited. Not wanting to raise my family in filth, I literally researched books on how to make the work easier. I asked friends, I read magazines, and I have a few suggestions.

If you love cleaning and have my mom's knack for it, skip this story, but if you're like me and you still wish things were clean even though they are not, here are five tips that have helped me feel like I'm in charge of the filth factor most days:

Take a big cardboard box and remove fifty knickknacks and other items cluttering your shelves and tables. It makes dusting a whole lot easier. When the season changes, switch the contents of the box. It's like getting new stuff!

Lose the top sheets on your bed. Instead, sew them into your covers or buy comforter covers. Get a down or polyester comforter, give away your bedspread and pillow shams, and making the bed now will take seconds instead of minutes. One quick shake of the comforter, and your bed will look neat and fresh! (The Europeans do this. I used to wonder why until I tried it!)

Make bigger meals. I chop a whole onion when I need only a fourth of one now, and store it in a sealed plastic container so I have it ready for later. I make meals big enough to feed us twice, and then serve leftovers or freeze the rest. I cook twice the rice and then combine whatever I have around on nights I'm too tired to cook and pour it over the rice as a sauce.

Keep a bottle of cleanser and some paper towels under the bathroom sink. When you finish brushing your teeth at night, squirt and wipe. Astonishing! The bathroom always looks clean. I only scrub once a week now—the rest of the time, it looks so good my mom could drop in without notice.

Enlist the aid of your children. Have them help not just in their rooms, but in the whole house. Believe it or not, they can be taught to scrape plates and put them in the dishwasher, to sweep the porch, or to vacuum the bedrooms. My daughter is a whiz at folding laundry. I feel faint with joy when she does it, but she can and sometimes does!

Using just one of these might unlock the key to your housecleaning stress. I eventually incorporated all of them, and although some days I think child protective services might secretly come and red tag my house for the filth factor, overall it's pretty nice here. Dingdong! Is that the doorbell? Oh, my gosh! It's my mom!

Girls Just Wanna Have Fun

Yard Sale—Recently married couple is combining households.
All duplicates will be sold, except children.
—Seen in the San Jose Mercury News

Women who miscalculate are called "mothers."
—Abigail van Buren (Dear Abby), columnist

Jeannie is in a tough position. She's got two little girls and shared custody with her ex, Tom, who works as a pharmacist. He's remarried to a woman substantially younger than him, who also has a little girl of her own.

"She's got this daughter who is nearly ten," Jeannie said. "She apparently got pregnant in high school at some party, according to what Tom said. I don't want her to be in my daughters' lives! What kind of example is that?"

Jeannie watched as Tom's new wife allowed all three girls to watch racy movies while they were together. The new wife allowed the girls to wear clothes that looked ridiculous on them, more suited for wild girls in their twenties.

"I called my attorney when the girls came home in black, fake leather miniskirts," Jeannie said. "He told me there was nothing I could do except maybe order psychological testing of all of us. It would cost me nearly $20,000, and since there was no abuse going on, it probably wouldn't change anything."

"My attorney said, "They have a right to raise the girls when they are with them any way they want, and although it upsets you, the best you can do is set a strong example at home."

Well, Jeannie is not about to accept anything easily, so she called the new wife. She asked her politely if she enjoyed her years as a single teen mother. The woman answered with a clear no. Jeannie mentioned, again politely, that perhaps watching movies that include adult sexual behavior and innuendoes and dressing like miniature adults was giving the children the wrong impression at an early age.

She held her breath. Not a member of the moral majority, but concerned about her daughters' futures, she was climbing right out on a limb for what she believed was right. As Jeannie tells me this story, I feel myself leaning forward in expectation. What did the young wife say?

"She said, 'You know, I never thought about it that way! My mom let me wear whatever I wanted, and never said a word. It makes sense, what you say.'"

Much to Jeannie's great surprise, the young woman stopped buying the little girls see-through shirts and miniskirts. She says her daughters report now that they are watching action movies at their dad's, like *Terminator* and such, which also alarms her but not as much as movies with blatant sexual behaviors.

"It's been two years now, and she seems to have really changed," Jeannie says. "I never thought she and I would be anything but adversaries, but I found out she's a sensible woman who also wants to be a good mother underneath it all."

Me and the Boyz

An ounce of mother is worth a ton of priest.
—Spanish proverb

Man was predestined to have free will.
—Hal Lee Luyah, as quoted in The 2,548 Best Things
Anybody Ever Said *by Robert Byrne*

Karen single-handedly raised two boys. Now one is in college, and one has just graduated from college. She's as proud as can be of both of them, since despite the harrowing teenage years, they've both grown into nice young men.

The older one, Scott, "was one of those kids who does everything right," Karen said. "He did his homework, he played in sports, he was nice and polite around the house, he got a part-time job and saved his money for college."

Apparently the younger one, Jeff, decided to make up for his brother's good behavior. "He got caught smoking pot in the bathroom at thirteen," Karen said, shaking her head. "He started ditching school, and he was mean when he was at home. Some nights he wouldn't come home at all, or if he did, I'd ask if he'd been drinking and he'd say 'No.' I knew he was lying to me, but didn't know what to do."

She enlisted the aid of the boys' father, and they went to the school counselor. When that didn't help, they went to a psychologist. Jeff's behavior was getting worse, not better. He was angry and confused.

Finally, he got violent at about fifteen. "That's the stage where parents kick the kids out," Karen said. "When they are just too much to handle anymore. He was stealing from me, and he was always angry; it was horrible!"

"But my ex and I had a meeting about it and decided not to let go of him. He had slipped so far away!" They went to another counselor who suggested a sort of juvenile delinquency camp on a remote island in Samoa. It cost a fortune, but the rigorous life straightened out many kids and turned them back into reasonable human beings.

Karen and her ex-husband, John, agreed that it was better to save their son than to abandon him. They scrimped and saved to pay the hefty tuition fees and shipped their son away, knowing there would be no contact for months except for form letters from the school. They prayed and wished and the months passed.

Finally, their son was allowed a telephone call for good behavior. He called his mom and cried into the phone, begging her to come and get him. He told stories of not being allowed to wear shoes, of being forced to eat sparse rations of horrible food, of sleeping in awful conditions. She stood strong and refused, although "My heart was aching to snatch him out of there."

Two years later, Jeff graduated from the island "prison camp," as he called it, and came home a new young man. He enrolled in college, helped with the dishes, and treated his mother with respect and gratitude. He was a new person, and Karen was glad she'd made the choice to save him rather than abandon him.

"It had gotten to a point where I had to look at him and say I really didn't like him anymore. But like and love are very different. If I'd thrown him away, and he admits it now, he would have ended up with a life in prison. But we hung on to him; we wouldn't let him slip over the edge, and he's a happy, grateful person today because of it."

Not having faced Karen's issues, I ask what it was like. "It was so hard! It was awful when he was with me, and awful when he called me suffering. It was extremely expensive to send him away—we had to do without a lot of things. We made it through, and now when he comes to visit me from college, and bends down to give me a kiss on the cheek, and says, 'Thanks for everything, Mom!' I know that I made the right choice. No kid is too incorrigible to be helped."

A Little Bit of Sunshine

Don't worry—be happy!—Bahamian lifestyle motto

Cindy never seems at a loss for help. She's one of those people who always has someone volunteering to baby-sit for her, to help her out with watching her dog when she's out of town, or to bring her a meal when she's sick. She's got invitations to holiday parties for the next four years straight.

I am one of the friends who contends with others for a chance to help Cindy out. She's a single mom with two little girls, one a preschooler. I could not figure out how she does it until I really started to concentrate on her methodology.

Cindy lives a very unstructured life. Oh, she gets the basics done, like taking one daughter to school and the other to preschool, but the rest of her life is lived loosely. She's one of those people you could call at 1 A.M. and ask if she's still up, and the answer would be yes, whether it was true or not. She apparently doesn't worry about anything. She doesn't spend a whole lot of time considering how she looks, or how other people evaluate her, or whether or not she's making enough money or being a good enough parent. In fact, she never seems to worry about anything. She's always happy with herself, with life, with her children. She is always ready for a good time—a trip to the bookstore, to the zoo, to the park. She is forever available herself, to help you out in a pinch.

She considers dozens of people her friends. Dozens and dozens. She has friends all over the country, from every city she's ever lived in, with whom she keeps in touch. She is playful in the extreme, and always ready to help anyone out any way she can. Even if you say no, it's always kind of her to offer.

She lives life with the vents wide open. It's interesting to analyze, because I am not much like her. But the different results are extraordinary. All of us lumped into Cindy's cheerful mix of "friends" would do anything for her, in part because we know she'd do anything for any of us, but also because she's such a delightful person to be around.

She has high integrity, but no fixed moral position on anything. She has enough money to have fun any time of the day or night, but little in savings. She is pure effervescence and laughter as well as very highly educated and quite intelligent. She's giving, loving, and extremely attentive to her young daughters. She always has time to play, with them or with her friends. She has an unending stream of answers to the question, "What should we do today?"

Cindy reminds me of the sunflowers that used to grow in my mother's garden in Chicago. She turns her face full strength to the sunshine in life, and pretty much doesn't pay attention to the darker things. As a result, people line up to bask in her friendship.

Daddy's Gone

Happy is the child whose father died rich. —*Russian proverb*

*My eleven-year-old daughter mopes around the house
all day waiting for her breasts to grow.*
—*Bill Cosby, actor, writer, celebrity*

Margaret's husband was a pilot for the Air Force in the 1950s. The family lived on a base in a snug little home. Four-year-old Susie and two-year-old Stuart were the darlings of their parents' lives. Life was good for Margaret and Ron.

Then one day, a soldier knocked on Margaret's door, and her life changed forever. Ron had just died in a crash!

Grief and sorrow overwhelmed her for the next few months, and family and friends gathered round to help in the first shocking days. Suddenly a single mother, Margaret's life went into its own tailspin.

The months became a year, and Margaret was still grieving. She was lonely, overworked, and although she had plenty of friends and companions around, she still had the responsibility for her growing children. "In the fifties, this just wasn't how life was supposed to be," she tells me, patting my hand with her worn, age-spotted one.

I ask her what she did, although I know the answer since her son, Stuart, is my friend. I'm sitting with Margaret on the deck of one of her and her husband's expansive homes looking over a vista of mountains and sea. We're on deck chairs that cost more than my car.

Margaret, still beautiful, began to be courted by a man who was good to the children. "It was hard to find a man who wanted a wife and two children right away," she told me. "But he was a good man, and he was kind to the kids, so when he asked, I said yes."

Now she had support and help again in a time when there were few options for single mothers in this country. Bob and Margaret raised the children as best they could, giving each a good start in the world. All these years later, I ask Margaret if she made the right decision. It doesn't seem to me that she and Bob are all that happy with one another. "I didn't have any choice," she says. "If I had been born in your time, I might have stayed single as you are doing," she comments. "But I thought Stuart needed a father, and there just weren't as many options for us."

I ask her if she did it because she needed the money. "No, not really," she says. "I had a job at a store and the military sent checks for the children, so we weren't hurting. It was just not done; it just wasn't how they did it, to raise children alone."

Margaret shifts in her chair and passes a hand absent-mindedly through her now-gray hair. "I suppose you young women now don't realize how lucky you are. You have every option in the world. You can stay single, you can remarry, you can live with someone, and you'll be fine. Society says nothing; the world is yours. You can choose whatever you wish. That's a lot of freedom, you know."

Margaret stops talking, and her eyes settle on some speck I cannot see on the distant hills. I know she's thinking about the choices she made. I think about what she said. I do have a lot of freedom. Perhaps I should be grateful for the options.

Dating Again

I used to be Snow White, but I drifted.
—Mae West, early feminist icon

It's been so long since I made love, I can't even remember
who gets tied up. —Joan Rivers, comedian

Dating again after a divorce can be a strange experience. Unlike dating before, now you get to contend with a baby-sitter waiting at home for you to return, and instead of feeling free to choose whoever pleases you, you must think about whether or not he will fit in with you and your child.

It changes the odds, and it changes the game. We've all met men who "don't date single mothers," men who want to date only single mothers, men who think that being divorced means we have baggage (that dreaded word!), and men who think that the only real women are women who have already been tempered by a long-term relationship.

Women seem to worry about whether or not their bodies look like they did when they were on the market the first time, before stretch marks; we worry about whether or not this person is a secret child molester, although he seems so nice; we wonder whether our kids should meet him and if they do, if they will like him.

Single Agains realize that the game is different this time. Single mothers will never be as footloose as they were the first time, and that's pretty much a fact of life. When I was writing my successful book about modern single woman-hood, *The Cult of the Born Again Virgin: How Single Women*

Can Reclaim Their Sexual Power, I interviewed nearly one hundred women on their attitudes about sexuality and relationships. Because I am one, many of the women I interviewed were single mothers.

"It's different now," Iris, a thirty-one-year-old single mom and realtor said, "because now I have to judge the man by much more serious criteria. Will he fit in with my son? Would he be a good provider? I never even thought of these things when I got involved with Jim!"

Chris, a forty-two-year-old single mom and stockbroker, said, "It's totally different now. I make my own money; I've had my children. There's no reason to want to be in a real relationship, plus I proved to myself that I don't really like being married."

I asked them and other women how they handle dating.

"I date when my kids are at their dad's."

"Date? That's a laugh! I don't have time to breathe!"

"Nobody asks me out any more. I think I have an invisible Do Not Disturb sign on my head."

"Guys just want one thing, and I'm not available to give it anymore."

"I'm dating someone right now. In a few more months, I'll introduce him to my kids. I'm nervous about that; they don't really know about him yet."

"I introduce my son to everyone I date. He's got better radar than I do. If he says the guy's a jerk, he usually turns out to be right!"

I observe that the point of dating needs to be clear in your mind. Ask yourself honestly what you want. Would you like a companion? Do you want to remarry? Are you just bored? Do you want a man to boost your self-esteem? Do you just want someone to play around with? Are you looking for someone to give you another baby or two? What's your objective?

Once you know what you want, really want, it makes it a lot easier to find. Whatever your answer today, it might change in six months. Life has a way of doing that. Single mothers have very limited amounts of time to spend with the wrong guys, or with guys whose relationship goals do not match ours. The difference is, now it is our game, and we're playing for very different stakes than we were before.

"I haven't got an evening to throw away on some moron," Deirdre tells me. "It's not worth the cost of the baby-sitter. I know precisely what I want, and I check out generally whether the guy's on the same page as I am before I say yes to any date."

Many women agreed with Deirdre: If you know what you want in advance, it's a heck of a lot easier to make sure the guy's in the same space as you. Ask questions before you invest precious time and energy. It's amazing how the doors open for she who knocks.

On Living Single

Love is being stupid together. —Paul Valery, French writer

Remember your dreams when you were a little girl? How you fantasized your life would be when you grew up? What kind of job did you want to have? Did you want to be a mommy or a ballerina or a veterinarian, or all three? Did you want to save the world or the whales?

Chances are, your life is a lot different than you imagined it was going to be. Richard Bolles, author of the international best-seller *What Color Is Your Parachute?*, writes that at age seven and eight we are usually pretty in touch with who we really are and what skills and dreams are our true selves.

Think back for a moment to yourself at that young age—third grade. It seems so long ago! Where did you live? What was your favorite toy? What color was your bedroom?

Think about what you wanted to become. Grab a piece of paper and write down what your dream was—what you wanted to be before the world started to color in it's own picture of who you should become. Use color and detail—describe exactly what you wanted. I wanted to look like Barbie, have her wardrobe, and be a writer. Getting one out of three isn't bad! With a little liposuction and some silicone, there's still hope (just kidding!).

Next write down all the things you wanted to try but haven't yet. Did you see *Fame* and want to take modern dance classes but never found the time? Did you want to watercolor? How about learning accounting, or flower arranging, or learning to sew or play the piano? What do you wish your parents had made you stick with when you were little? What lessons did you always want to take?

What impractical and practical things do you wish you could have learned so far? Would you like to have set your life up so you could learn another language? Did you always want your scuba diving certification?

List everything, no matter how silly it seems, that you wish you had taken time for along the path or that you'd like to do "someday."

Done? Good. Now circle the top three. The three that would be truly interesting to learn about, things that would really add color to your life if only there was a way to do them right now.

Now imagine, if you will, that you only have one life to live. Imagine how sorry you'd feel for your child if he or she had passed by the things that she or he really wanted to do in life. Imagine how sad it would be to be an old woman, nearly dead, angry, sad, or a bitter martyr over all the things that she "could have done" or "could have had" if it weren't for her children in her way.

Now pretend you have decided to live the life you've been given and show your children an example of a dynamic, connected woman who balances her own needs with those of her children. Imagine you look in the mirror as an old woman and see a face that is lovingly wrinkled from a life well spent, full of vitality and zest. Think how much more this old woman's children will want to visit her than the other embittered martyr.

Today is the day you can start living despite the fact you are a single mother with seventeen little kids and three full-time jobs. Today is the day you can start living your dreams instead of wishing things were different. Choose just one of your top three wishes, if you don't have time for them all, and do it. Call and find out how much just one dance lesson would be, if that's your dream. I know a woman who did this and fell so in love with it after one lesson that she started taking a brown bag lunch to work to afford more lessons.

I've taken classes when I couldn't afford a baby-sitter by calling the instructor, asking if I can bring a quiet child, and then bringing enough snacks and toys to entertain my daughter. I've swapped childcare with other parents, and I've hired teenagers to baby-sit.

Make the phone call today, or go to the library and check out a book on the subject. Subscribe to a magazine related to your dream—I subscribed to *Skin Diver* magazine for years before I had enough money to take diving lessons!

By making a move toward something you think is fun, you are carving out a life for yourself. It's amazing how this transforms your week, your attitude about your kids, your attitude at work, your attitude about everything. One bright spot, one hour of following your dreams every week, could be enough to change the whole picture of your life!

Flab, Stretch Marks, and Me

In most countries, sex is a fact. In America, it is an obsession. —Marlene Deitrich, actor

The following is a true story, and it is definitely stranger than fiction. It changed my attitude about my body, and about other women's bodies, forever. We all know by now that other people easily pick up on our attitude about our bodies and about ourselves. This explains why some people get great service, get to return the item even without a receipt, get the best parking spaces, while other people don't get any of these things.

Men also pick up on our radar about ourselves and our bodies. Most women know that, and we also pick up on them, so it all works out. This is terrific, of course, but I for one look at the covers of the fashion mags when I am in line at the grocery store. I look at their hair and their makeup and their exposed cleavages, and I know I do not look like that. I can buy all the magazines I want about having a flat stomach and no butt and firm thighs in two-and-a-half-minutes per day, and frankly, it just ain't gonna happen.

So here's the story. I went on a wilderness girl-bonding sort of retreat one summer when my daughter was on vacation with her father. I didn't know any of the other women who would be attending, and I was assigned a bunkmate for the trip, sort of a buddy. Her name was Janine.

This woman was lovely, with an exquisite figure and a porcelain doll face. Her soft wavy, brown hair was perfect, and I saw her without makeup for most of the trip and still was awed by how beautiful she was.

Janine had come to the camp with four other women. They all lived in Las Vegas. They were all strippers!

Because of my bunkmate, I hung out with her and her friends. We'd sit around the campfire chatting after a hard day of wilderness survival stuff. After a few days, there were about a dozen of us who hung out together in the cold evenings, burning hot on one side as we faced the fire, freezing on the other.

As such things go, the experience invited questions and opened doors to honesty. I asked Janine and her friends what it was like to be a stripper. They told us stories of what it was like, and I asked about the bodies. "All of you seem perfect physically," although I'd never seen any of them except Janine in less than a ski jacket, jeans, and boots. "Are all strippers perfect?"

They all laughed at the same time at my question. It was more naive than I thought. Marcie said, "Oh, no way! One of my club's most successful strippers must be a size 14! She's got short brown hair, and she just sort of knows how to show it to the best advantage."

I was thinking I could never be a stripper, especially not if I were a size 14, when Janine said, "At my club there's a girl who got into a car accident, and she has a scar on her leg. The guys who come in think it's cool. She's really popular."

The four of them went on to name the defects and commonness of themselves and their comrades at the strip joints they worked at. The rest of us sat spellbound by their tales. The men seemed to be interested in all different sorts of women—big, fat, tall, masculine faces, feminine faces, big boobs, no boobs, big butts, no butts, cellulite, scar tissue, stretch marks, athletic, boyish, and everything else you could think of.

Finally, one of my other non-stripper companions took the words out of all our mouths when she said, "I could never be a stripper! I don't feel confident naked!"

Janine laughed. "That's the whole point," she said. "It's her confidence in herself that makes the best strippers so successful and desirable to the customers. If you've got confidence in how you look, or if you can fake it, you're suddenly desirable. There are some really pretty girls who don't make it because they think they're ugly in some secret way."

Now while I doubt any of their audience took this as career advice, I did take it to heart as personal advice. Perhaps you should, too, because I've tested it and it proves true. If you walk into a room imagining you are the most desirable woman there, it's amazing how much attention you get. If you walk in wishing you were ten pounds lighter, or had different colored hair, or had remembered to paint your nails, you somehow signal to the room that you aren't all that confident in yourself. It's odd how it works, but a bunch of sweet, honest stripper girls changed the way I present myself in public. My results have been dramatic, and the two other women from the trip who I know tried it too report the same results.

Men aren't interested in a fashion model; they're interested in a woman who is confident enough in herself to move with poise, speak with grace, and take a conversational interest in the other person. Astonishing! Test it; it works.

The Sky's the Limit

"I've been eating the way I like for eighty years," my grandfather said, slathering a piece of bread with butter to accompany a one-inch-thick slab of canned ham. "What the hell difference is it going to make if I start living like a health nut now?
—Alexander Keller, the author's grandfather

When my grandfather was eighty-four years old, he told me he was so sick he couldn't walk across my father's house all at once anymore. He'd been living with Dad and his wonderful wife for years. Knowing the end was nigh, my daughter and I made the trip to my father's house in remote Missouri, to visit my grandfather for the last time.

I found my grandfather much as he had described himself, but more melancholy. He'd always been a great wit, and had the most extraordinary sense of humor if you were paying attention to his words. But on this occasion, although his eyes misted at the sight of me, his favorite grandchild, he told me he was eager to die. He told me, "Old age isn't all that it's cracked up to be, kid." We smiled and hugged.

The next morning, Grandpa and I stood in the house at the big picture window and watched my dad and my daughter make the long walk down the driveway to cross the street to the park. Grandpa strained to see them, watching with deep joy and, I suspect, some sense of security that the world would go on without him. Perhaps he was remembering the many times he'd walked me to a park to push me endlessly on a swing a generation ago. I watched him watch them and wondered what it was like to wait to die.

Suddenly, I had an idea. "C'mon, Gramps!" I said with enthusiasm. "Let's go to the park!" He complained and protested, but I got him out of the house and into his beat-up old van. I drove him across the street and parked on the basketball court, just a hundred feet or so from the swings where my father, sure enough, was pushing his own granddaughter. Two grandpas, two granddaughters.

My eighty-four-year-old grandfather sat on the carousel and my eight-year-old daughter pushed him in circles while he made wisecracks about needing to "take some of that medicine that keeps you from getting dizzy." He stood up and appeared to stumble, so my dad and I rushed to his side. But he was laughing! "I tricked you both!" he cried as he headed off for the slide.

He climbed the tower of the curly slide, with my daughter egging him on. My dad followed him up, to make sure he didn't fall backward. What kind of an old man climbs up a slide like a kid? My grandfather, that's what kind.

My daughter and I yelled encouragement from the ground. My grandfather stood at the top and announced that this was It, and he was wishing us all a good life, because he knew he wouldn't make it to the bottom. He was laughing as he spoke and so were we, as he admonished us to take care of one another. It was all done in fun, and he complained loudly about us "making him" do this, and asked why were we "trying to kill him." We laughed until we nearly fell over. It had been his idea after all.

I took lots of pictures. I snapped his farewell President Getting off Air Force One wave as he prepared to descend, and then, whoosh! Grandpa slid down the slide to the cheers of his family and loud whooping from his great granddaughter.

By the time he got to the bottom, his white hair had blown straight up into a punk rocker style, and he looked shaken but proud. He hugged us all and made his way to the bench to watch the rest of our antics for half an hour before we all drove home across the street in his dented old van.

For the rest of the visit, he alternated between telling us what fun he'd had and how he couldn't understand why we were all trying to kill him since there wasn't much left to inherit. But I could tell he was proud of himself. He'd sucked the last drop out of life and would die the way he lived—bold, adventurous, and beloved.

My grandfather died that autumn, about five months later. It's easy to say now, but I knew he was gone before they called to say he died. He left a mark on all our lives. His example is like an indelible, permanent marker scrawled across our hearts. He drew a huge smiley face, with a tongue poking out!

What kind of legacy am I creating for my child, who will raise my grandchildren? What kind of example am I setting? When I die, will my descendants remember me as bitter and struggling or as joyful and lively to the end? How will yours remember you? It's all up to us. Let us savor life while we live and walk boldly in the direction of our dreams.

Bibliography

Bolles, Richard Nelson. *What Color Is Your Parachute?* Berkeley: Ten Speed Press, 1996.

Breathnach, Sarah Ban. *Simple Abundance: A Daybook of Comfort and Joy.* New York: Warner Books, 1995.

Byron, Robert. *The 2,548 Best Things Anybody Ever Said.* New York: Galahad Books, 1996.

Csikszentmihalyi, Mihaly. *Finding Flow: The Psychology of Engagement with Everyday Life.* New York: Basic Books, 1997.

Fuller, Cheri. *How to Motivate Your Kids from Crayons to Career: How to Boost Your Child's Learning and Achievement without Pressure.* Tulsa, OK: Honor Books, 1990.

James, John W., and Frank Cherry. *The Grief Recovery Handbook: A Step-by-Step Program for Moving Beyond Loss.* New York: Perennial Library, 1988.

Keller, Wendy. *The Cult of the Born Again Virgin: How Single Women Can Reclaim Their Sexual Power.* Deerfield Beach, FL: Health Communications, Inc., 1999. www.KellerMedia.com

Mitchell, W. *It's Not What Happens To You, It's What You Do About It.* Santa Barbara, CA: Phoenix Press, 1997.

Nietzche, Friedrich Wilhelm, et al. Philosophical Writings: German Library, XXXX Continuum Publishing Group, 1995.

Scott, Susan. *Create the Love of Your Life.* New York: Zebra Books, 1993.

Stanley, Thomas J., Ph.D. and William D. Danko Ph.D. *The Millionaire Next Door: The Surprising Secrets of America's Wealthy.* Marietta, GA: Longstreet Press, 1996.

A Note from the Author

Thanks for reading this book. I hope you enjoyed it. My daughter and I live with Lucky, our German sheperd, five goldfish won at carnivals, and a mouse named Penelope. All of us would love to hear from you. If you enjoyed this book, and have any comments, questions, or thoughts to share, please e-mail me at SoloMothers@aol.com. I send you my very best wishes for a wonderful time with your children while you are a single mom.

About the Author

Wendy Keller is the author of *The Cult of the Born Again Virgin* and 21 other books. She is also the founder of the ForthWrite Literary Agency and Speakers Bureau. She has appeared on dozens of national television shows, including Dateline NBC, Crosstalk, Politically Incorrect, and MSNBC. She teaches seminars for women on self-esteem and lives in Malibu, California. To contact Ms. Keller about speaking events or to find out more information about her agency and bureau, please visit her website: www.KellerMedia.com.

About the Press

Wildcat Canyon Press publishes books that embrace such subjects as friendship, spirituality, women's issues, and home and family, all with a focus on self-help and personal growth. Great care is taken to create books that inspire reflection and improve the quality of our lives. Our books invite sharing and are frequently given as gifts.

For a catalog of our publications, please write:
Wildcat Canyon Press
2716 Ninth Street
Berkeley, California 94710
Phone: (510) 848-3600
Fax: (510) 848-1326
or visit our website at www.wildcatcanyon.com